Books of Merit

Roots of Empathy

ROOTS OF EMPATHY

Changing the World
Child by Child

———————

MARY GORDON

Thomas Allen Publishers
Toronto

Library and Archives Canada Cataloguing in Publication

Gordon, Mary, 1947–
Roots of empathy : changing the world, child by child / Mary Gordon.

Includes bibliographical references and index.

ISBN 0-88762-128-7

1. Caring in children.
2. Empathy.
3. Aggressiveness in children—Prevention.
4. Violence in children—Prevention.
5. Child rearing.
I. Title.

HQ769.G67 2005   649'.7
C2004-902544-9

Cover photo: Melanie Gordon

Song lyrics (p. xvii): "Turn this World Around (A Song for Nelson Mandela)."
Words and music by Raffi, Michael Creber © 2001 Homeland Publishing.
A division of Troubadour Records Ltd. All rights reserved.
Reprinted by permission.

The publisher gratefully acknowledges the support of
the Ontario Arts Council for its publishing program.

We acknowledge the support of the Canada Council for the Arts, which
last year invested $21.7 million in writing and publishing throughout Canada.

We acknowledge the support of the Government of Ontario through the
Ontario Media Development Corporation's Ontario Book Initiative.

We acknowledge the financial support of the Government of Canada through the Book
Publishing Industry Development Program (BPIDP) for our publishing activities.

09 08 07 06 05   1 2 3 4 5

Printed and bound in Canada

To my parents, George and Helen Dyer,
who loved me well and would have been
very happy to read this book.

Acknowledgements

To the thousands of parents who, with their babies, have volunteered the gift of their time to the Roots of Empathy family, thank you.

To all of the Roots of Empathy instructors, mentors and trainers, who have shared their stories, thank you. To the Roots of Empathy staff, whose energy and commitment light each day, thank you. A special note of love and thanks to the memory of Dr. David (Dan) Offord, a founding board member who served up to the time of his death last year. Dr. Dan's influence led Roots of Empathy to become a research-based program. A big thank you to Merrill Lynch, our first major corporate sponsor in Canada.

To our Board of Directors who provide unerring direction and support for the dream and the everyday construction of our yellow brick road, thank you.

To Susan Cook, and her unfailing good humour, who, more than anyone else, has made this book happen—many thanks.

To Teresa Pitman, who was helpful with the framework and early stages of the book, thank you.

To Patrick Crean and Jim Allen, of Thomas Allen Publishers, who had faith in me and this project, your patience and encouragement during the writing of this book showed me what a civilized world publishing can be, thank you.

To Joan Green, who offered valuable feedback to the early drafts of the book and spent long hours in discussion with me. Thank you.

To Heather McFarlane and Christopher Sarson; old friends, supporters and co-conspirators in the early development of Roots of Empathy.

To all of those who helped in many ways to deliver this story, thank you.

To my husband, Keith, for being my trusted sounding board. To my daughter Melanie, for her wise counsel and the photograph which graces the cover of this book. To my son Eric, who inspires me on a regular basis, thank you.

All proceeds from the sales of this book will be directed to Roots of Empathy to support the development of empathy in children so that they may change the world, child by child.

Contents

Foreword

I grew up in Newfoundland, raised in a large loving family with three generations under one roof. My parents were passionate about social justice. One night when I was six and my sister Susan was eight, my father put an empty tin on the dinner table while we were eating and put some coins in it. He explained to us that we couldn't have the black patent leather, Mary-Jane party shoes we wanted, because the money would go to buy shoes for little girls in India who didn't have any.

It was well known by the local jail population that when you got released, you could go up to Mrs. Dyer's (my mother's) for a hot meal. I remember being invited to make our guest welcome by sitting at the card table in the hall to share a conversation as he ate his meal. From my mother, we learned about the dignity every person was entitled to, regardless of circumstances.

I offer these stories by way of explaining the power of family and the impact that incidents in everyday life can have in shaping the values we carry forever. I was picked up rather than put down when I faltered as a child, and that helped me to trust myself.

The journey that brought me to Roots of Empathy has been rich and winding, and recurring themes have appeared along the way:

The Importance of Family: I witnessed intergenerational cycles of violence first-hand when I worked with families caught in the cycle of child abuse, neglect or domestic violence. The pervasiveness of these social ills can be addressed when we look at the common denominator of these ills—the absence of empathy. As children develop empathy, they become more adept at finding the humanity in one another. Without empathy, we can't get to conflict resolution, altruism or peace. There are two overarching understandings from working with families; first, children develop within the culture of their family and we need to work with that rather than against it. Second, it is the relationships rather than the structure of families that count.

The Privilege of Working with Children: My work with children who had been victims of abuse or neglect, who lived in hostels, who lived with the unpredictability of addict parents, taught me that they love, purely and without judgment, and have an infinite capacity for forgiveness. All children can teach us lessons of loyalty and acceptance. Working with little children as a kindergarten teacher, I was overwhelmed by both their strength and vulnerability. I was amazed by the honest way they wore their feelings in their behaviour. All those who have the opportunity to work with young children touch the future. Unfortunately in North America, we live in a child-illiterate society where child-care workers are undervalued, and those who parent children at home are often dismissed as marking time until they get back into the workforce. My hope is that this book will support the vital importance of children and all those who are involved with their development.

The Universal Need for Love and Belonging: When I worked with parents who had abused their children, it was very clear that they were not the monsters that the public thought they were. These parents were all desperately seeking acceptance, recognition and love, but their life experiences had left them devoid of empathy. All too often, when children or youth are made to feel that they don't belong, their response is a desire to "get even." The headlines capture the most dramatic examples of youth "getting even" in the statistics of suicide, aggression and murder.

A realization of the devastating impact of neglect or abuse on the lives of children, and alarm over societal violence, which is often the result of marginalized childhoods and poor parenting, set me on a path to find ways to break this cycle. This was my initial motivation; however, the lessons Roots of Empathy teaches reach out to touch all children and strengthen their capacity to engage with the world using empathy.

The Value of Public Education: My first career as a kindergarten teacher introduced me to the power of education as an equalizer. Public education is the basis of a healthy democracy. Working in schools, whether in school-based parenting centres or classrooms, I saw how crucial it is that we teach children to ask questions and help them find their voice. Voice is bound up in their confidence and feelings of self-worth and is key to their future as citizens who will take their place in a democratic society. We need to use the evidence about how children truly learn, not through telling and yelling, but through meaningful experiences that engage both the mind and the heart. Roots of Empathy addresses the affective side of learning, the part that fails to get measured in the way math and reading are. The goal of education is broader than creating job-ready youth—it involves nurturing individuals who can be publicly useful and personally fulfilled. Education has a responsibility to develop citizens. Students who have good job skills but poor social and emotional skills may get a job, but will have trouble keeping it or getting promoted.

The Power of the Arts: Art is a vehicle that allows children the expression of a depth and complexity of emotion beyond what their words can convey. Music, art and drama are portals to emotional literacy, a skill we all need to form strong relationships throughout our lives. In my work with struggling parents I have always found that paint, permission and friendship can heal and connect. The coloured insert of children's art has been included in this book to share the children's insights. In their art, children speak to themselves as they paint what they feel instead of what they see. If we watch carefully, we may just learn from them.

Though I am a trained teacher, I find that I am also a trained learner, and my teachers have often been the most unlikely people. I believe that children have a great deal to teach us, and Roots of Empathy is a journey where children frequently lead the way. I invite you to walk with the many children you will meet in this book and discover how they are changing our world.

I have written this book for everyone who touches the lives of children—not just the "usual suspects" like parents and teachers, but also those who work in organizations that provide programs or services to children. Children's perspectives are important, and in the following pages, you will hear from them directly. The names of the children in this book are not real, but their stories are.

During the Nuremberg Trials, one of the judges described the war crimes as a failure of empathy. Yet, in recent history, the world's response to the tsunami of 2004 was a triumph of empathy. Normally, our differences define and separate us, providing the fodder for marginalization, bullying and exclusion. If we were to listen to the language of the groups who are in a "hate relationship" with another group, they somehow manage to speak of the other group as less human—or so different that there can be no basis for human exchange. The children described in this book are able to see beyond differences to commonalities; and the baby who visits these children in the classroom acts as a catalyst for developing empathy. Empathy is integral to solving conflict in the family, schoolyard, boardroom and war room. The ability to take the perspective of another person, to identify commonalities through our shared feelings is the best peace pill we have.

The Roots of Empathy classroom is creating citizens of the world—children who are developing empathic ethics and a sense of social responsibility that takes the position that we all share the same lifeboat. These are the children who will build a more caring, peaceful and civil society, child by child.

Beloved children's entertainer and child advocate Raffi wrote and performed a song for Nelson Mandela with a chorus that echoes, "Turn, turn, turn, turn this world around for the children, turn this world around." This power—to "turn this world around"—is exactly what I believe our children can do.

Roots of Empathy

SECTION ONE

Roots of Empathy

1

FROM A TINY SEED

IMAGINE A GRADE 3 CLASSROOM. Recess has just ended and the children are shouting across the room to one another, still caught up in the game that they played outside. The teacher is about to raise her hand—the cue for them to settle down. The Roots of Empathy instructor has arrived and is spreading a green blanket on the floor. It is as if a spell has been cast. Quietly, the children arrange themselves cross-legged on the floor around the blanket. The hush in the room is palpable. The classroom door opens. A young mother is standing there with her five-month-old baby. The baby is wriggling in his mother's arms; his legs are drumming against his mother's body. He is clearly excited. Without prompting, the children break out in a greeting song: "Hello,

Tomas, how are you? How are you? How are you? Hello, Tomas, how are you? How are you today?"

Tomas and his mother walk around the green blanket greeting each child in turn. Mom sits down and places Tomas on his tummy; the children wait eagerly to see what he will do. It is time to ask Mom what life with Tomas has been like over the month since Tomas last visited the classroom. Has the baby laughed yet? Has Tomas tried any food? Can he roll over yet? Did his first tooth come in?

The instructor kneels on the blanket and holds up a toy. It is one that Tomas has not shown interest in before. It's colourful, it has bold patterns, it has different textures and it makes a delightful jingling sound: a multisensory learning tool. In an earlier class the instructor has taught the students that babies learn through their senses, that neurons form synaptic connections from environmental stimuli. As the children watch Tomas's face and body react to hearing the jingle, they snap their fingers—demonstrating the surge of electricity that is connecting neurons in Tomas's brain. The children appreciate that Tomas has to coordinate vision and hearing to find the toy, just as they had to coordinate balancing and pedalling when learning to ride a two-wheeler. They continue watching closely as Tomas tries to locate where the jingle is coming from and, as his eyes find the toy, they snap their fingers again, but this time the snapping is accompanied by excited shouts of encouragement: "Way to go, Tomas!" Tomas's brain is growing. And the children catch that moment of growth.

Tomas's mother is impressed by the interest the children take in her son's development and moved by their obvious excitement at every new thing Tomas learns.

The children have spent time with the instructor the previous week preparing for Tomas's visit, predicting what he will be able to do. They will spend time in the week after Tomas's visit exploring what they learned and connecting it to their own development and feelings. And then the big leap—gaining an understanding of their classmates' feelings.

This is a snapshot of a few moments in a Roots of Empathy classroom. Tomas and his mother will visit this class every month for the school year. The children will be coached by the instructor to observe the parent–child relationship, the baby's development, the baby's temperament, their own temperament and that of their classmates. They will learn about infant safety and issues that have an impact on their own well-being and security. They will learn how an understanding of temperament and gaining insights into their own emotions and those of others leads to empathy and builds rich human relationships.

Sowing Seeds of Empathy

Darren was the oldest child I ever saw in a Roots of Empathy class. He was in Grade 8 and had been held back twice. He was two years older than everyone else and already starting to grow a beard. I knew his story: his mother had been murdered in front of his eyes when he was four years old, and he had lived in a succession of foster homes ever since. Darren looked menacing because he wanted us to know he was tough: his head was shaved except for a ponytail at the top and he had a tattoo on the back of his head.

The instructor of the Roots of Empathy program was explaining to the class about differences in temperament that day. She invited the young mother who was visiting the class with Evan, her six-month-old baby, to share her thoughts about her baby's temperament. Joining in the discussion, the mother told the class how Evan liked to face outwards when he was in the Snugli and didn't want to cuddle into her, and how she would have preferred to have a more cuddly baby. As the class ended, the mother asked if anyone wanted to try on the Snugli, which was green and trimmed with pink brocade. To everyone's surprise, Darren offered to try it, and as the other students scrambled to get ready for lunch, he strapped it on. Then he asked if he could put Evan in. The mother was a little apprehensive, but she handed him the baby, and he put Evan in, facing towards his chest. That wise little baby snuggled right in, and Darren took him into a quiet corner and rocked back and forth with the baby in his arms for several minutes. Finally, he came back to where the mother and the Roots of Empathy instructor were waiting and he asked: "If nobody has ever loved you, do you think you could still be a good father?"

A seed has been sown here. This boy, who has seen things no child should see, whose young life has been marked by abandonment, who has struggled to the age of fourteen with scarcely a memory of love, has seen a glimmer of hope. Through these moments of contact with the uncritical affection of the baby, an adolescent boy has caught an image of himself as a parent that runs counter to his loveless childhood. The baby may have changed the trajectory of this youth's future by allowing him to see the humanity in himself. For eight years now I have seen the lights go on for children in Roots of Empathy classes as we give them a working model of loving and responsive parenting and an opportunity to interact with an infant in the first year of life.

Roots of Empathy is a program for school-aged children that involves them, right in their own classrooms, in the human dynamic of the parent–baby relationship. It is a program that has the capacity to instill in our children a concept of themselves as strong and caring individuals, to give them an understanding of empathic parenting and to inspire in them a vision of citizenship that can change the world. The program puts relationships at the centre of what creates a civil society, whether that society is a small classroom, the whole school, the community, the country or our ever-shrinking globe. The relationship story is made real for children as they connect with a baby and parent who are regular visitors to their classroom during the first year of the baby's life. The relationship between the parent and child is a template for positive, empathic human relationships. What the children learn here has universal and far-reaching implications: it shapes how they deal with each other today, and it lays a foundation for their future as parents and citizens.

The children involved in the program and the adults who support it invariably come to know what can only be described as the wisdom of the baby. The baby's behaviour and the emotions she expresses are spontaneous and pure; they are not hidden behind layers of socialization and the biases we acquire as we grow up. To the baby every child in the class is a new experience and she is ready to engage with all of them. In her world view there are no popular children and no nasty children. What the baby does see, over and over again, are the children who are unhappy or troubled, and she usually reaches out to them. Children who have felt alienated or excluded are drawn into a circle of inclusion through the empathic contact made by the baby.

Roots of Empathy places babies in the role of teachers because babies love without borders or definition. Babies respond intuitively to love. They are blind to differences as defined by the world. It is only when young children learn from the adult world that some are more worthy than others, because of some perceived difference, that we see the unfolding of the intergenerational legacy of racism, classism and a host of other "isms."

David was nine years old and had a form of autism. His parents shared with me that David had never been invited to a birthday party by any of his classmates until the year that Roots of Empathy came into his classroom. During this year he was invited to three birthday parties. Also in this year David's feelings about himself and school took a 180-degree turn. No medicine ever affected his life as much as the inclusive response of his classmates. This changed behaviour comes from the children's new understanding of the pain of exclusion and the importance of including someone who is different. This is the transformative power of the Roots of Empathy program.

Of all the literacies of childhood, emotional literacy is the most fundamental. Feelings define our similarity as humans. Our emotions are universal. The ability to find the humanity in one another will change the way that we relate to one another. It can have a huge impact on the family, by interrupting patterns of child abuse and neglect that are so often repeated through parenting in the next generation. It can have an impact on policies that lead us into conflict or compromise. It can have an impact on our very identity as citizens of the world.

Teaching children emotional literacy and developing their capacity to take the perspective of others are key steps towards collaboration and civility; they are indispensable steps towards preventing aggressive and bullying behaviours. This is borne out by the research that has been conducted on the effectiveness of the Roots of Empathy program. When children learn to draw the curtain on cruelty, they will not condone classmates bullying others. It is remarkable to see children standing up courageously to a bully. There are no onlookers or bystanders in the program, as children realize they have a responsibility to one another because they understand what it feels like to be frightened or humiliated or even physically hurt. As children develop empathy it seems to come ready-made with courage and imagination. Children understand marginalization and issues of social justice in a clear and uncluttered way.

At one school I visited, ten-year-old Jessie was lining up with the rest of her classmates to go out for lunch when one of the boys grabbed a hat right off the head of another boy. It's the kind of behaviour that is repeated every day, in every school, in every community. As adults, we often ignore it or simply sigh with exasperation. But the truth is, it has the effect of making the other child feel helpless and making him a target for ridicule.

If you have empathy, you understand how that victim feels. In the midst of a crowd of onlookers, he has to either work up the courage to retrieve the hat or ignore the taunting boy, and carry the humiliation and loss of dignity silently into the playground. Jessie stepped out of the line-up and confronted the young fellow who took the hat and said, calmly but firmly, "Give him back his hat." The boy looked around the line-up, weighing the reactions of the others. What he saw, I imagine, was that others in the group empathized with his victim; it could just as easily have been them. Finally he said, "Oh, take your stupid hat," and gave it back. Not the most gracious response, perhaps, but a moral victory had been won. Jessie had acted on her feeling of empathy and the human right of that child not to be humiliated. Every child in the class had been given a new promise—that these small acts of cruelty would not be tolerated, and that they would find support if they, too, were victims. An incident like this prompts us to see that sometimes the bravest advocates wear size three sneakers.

The seeding of citizenship in the classroom is aimed at creating a level of civility in the community and building the foundation for breaking intergenerational cycles of indifference and apathy. They may be students in the classroom but they are the parents, policy-makers and electorate of the future. Roots of Empathy creates the conditions for good citizenship to grow in much the same way that farmers who are not responsible for manufacturing crops are responsible for creating the conditions under which crops can thrive. The interactive, emotionally validating conditions of the Roots of Empathy classroom create the safe backdrop for children to become all that they might be.

There is an unexpected magnificence in our children and an underestimated power in their ability to change our world for the better. It is through our children that we can go beyond the frontiers of science and technology to explore the recesses of the human heart. We have managed to harness the power of the wind, the sun and the water, but have yet to appreciate the power of our children to effect social change.

A major cause of many of the conflicts in the world is our intolerance of difference. On the world stage, differences provide the justification for genocide and war, or failure to respond in times of disaster and disease. Over the ages, differences in religion, nationality, race, culture or language have been the cause for condoned slaughter. On the playground, differences become a target for bullies, for in the difference lies the vulnerability. Bullies capitalize on differences in their victims, whether it is that the child is shorter, fatter, less popular or less athletic. The current epidemic of bullying across schools and communities in North America is on the radar screen of parents, educators, children's mental health workers and the justice system.

Roots of Empathy is a pedagogy of hope, because in our children we have an opportunity to create a new order where our differences can be acknowledged and respected but our similarities will be our uniting force. The program coaches children to build a caring classroom as they become able to see their shared humanity—the idea that "what hurts my feelings is likely to hurt your feelings." The program is based on the idea that if we are able to take the perspective of the Other we will notice and appreciate our commonalities and we will be less likely to allow differences to cause us to marginalize, hate or hurt each other.

The Roots of Empathy Year

When Tomas, whom you met at the beginning of this chapter, visited the classroom, his visit was just one of twenty-seven sessions that make up our program. There are nine themes and each theme revolves around three classroom visits each month led by a trained and certified instructor. The centrepiece of each theme is a visit from the Roots of Empathy family. This visit is preceded by a preparation session with the instructor, and is followed by another class to discuss the visit and work on activities that reinforce what the children are learning in each theme.

Our curriculum is specialized for four different age groups: kindergarten, Grades 1 to 3, Grades 4 to 6, and Grades 7 to 8. For example, five-year-olds will learn the language of their feelings and be given many opportunities to be involved in physical activities. This part of the program respects the five-year-olds' need to be actively engaged and to speak about their own experiences. Ten-year-olds also learn the language of their feelings, but in addition they learn about the contagion of feelings, and the confusion of having many feelings at the same time. Ten-year-olds revel in understanding the mystery of competing emotions, but five-year-olds would not be able to understand the concepts.

The visits with the baby are naturally greeted with high levels of enthusiasm by the students;[1] however, the rich content of the pre- and post-family-visit classes engages students in discussions and activities related to themes such as emotions, safety and communicating. In the pre-family-visit class the instructor introduces the theme, links it to the stages of baby's development and elicits from the children predictions about what their particular baby will be able to do when she comes to visit. After the visit, the students consolidate what they have learned. This includes group discussions, artwork, drama, journal writing or perhaps a math exercise. In a pre-visit session, for example, the students might practise ways to hold a baby, using a lifelike doll. In a post-visit session, they might discuss their own experiences with childhood fears or their memories of favourite lullabies. The program draws out the generosity of children as the activities in the curriculum invite them to use art, music, drama and song as vehicles for presenting the baby and parent with classroom gifts.

The Roots of Empathy curriculum aligns with the regular school curriculum in many areas of learning. The work the instructor does with the students, particularly in the sessions held before and after the baby visit, touches on social studies, art, science and mathematics. Perhaps the strongest curriculum link of all is the way the program reinforces the school's literacy goals through the many discussions and writing assignments built into each session. The instructor uses well-known children's literature to illustrate emotions such as loneliness and sadness and to underscore themes such as inclusion and bullying. And, without fail, the stories stimulate perspective-taking and open a floodgate to rich discussion and enhanced understanding. During many of the pre- and post-visit sessions, the instructors read aloud the books that have been chosen to prompt deeper discussion around the theme for the month. In some instances, picture books are used even with Grade 7 and 8 students. With students of this age, the focus is on coaching them to take the perspective of the younger children in the stories; instructors are trained to use the theme and drama of the books as jumping-off points for older children to explore the issues that concern them.

Music is an important element, too. The children sing welcome songs and good-bye songs at the beginning and ending of each visit, and take part in action songs (such as "Itsy Bitsy Spider" or "This Little Piggy") as they interact with the baby. Even for older children, any self-consciousness they initially feel about singing a nursery song soon falls away as they get caught up in the baby's energetic reactions to familiar tunes.

The activities that are threaded through the program can be used in many ways, and often, long after the instructor is gone, teachers extend the Roots of Empathy learning experiences into regular classroom plans.

This program is given to the classroom teacher as a gift. The instructor who brings the program into the classroom is also often a gift—of agencies in the community of the school. These agencies fund the instructional time of the instructors, who are frequently on the staff of the agencies. The extensive training and mentoring provided to instructors by the Roots of Empathy organization is considered by the agencies to be valuable professional development. Classroom teachers have an opportunity to be with their students and observe them in a completely different light during the Roots of Empathy classes. Teachers comment on the emotional development of their students over the course of the year, in particular the kindness they witness, which had not been in evidence before. Many teachers tell us this is their most enjoyable time with the students and that the program positively changes the tone of the classroom.

The students witness the baby grow up in front of their eyes. They become solicitous of this baby and become advocates for all babies. They become part of an authentic dialogue with the Roots of Empathy parent and get insight into the joys and worries of being a parent. In the visits where the family is not present, students explore the connection between the baby's development and their own development; the connections between the baby's feelings and their own feelings. For example, when the baby struggles to sit up without support, and consistently falls over, the children discuss their frustration in baseball games as they try to hit the ball and can't get the bat to connect fast enough. The shared experience of seeing the baby struggle also allows the instructor to draw the analogy with the frustration the children feel when their schoolwork does not come easily. The discussion held in the classroom brings out into the open the negative feelings many children experience silently. The children develop strategies for helping one another, and give themselves permission to struggle openly, and to feel safe and not vulnerable when asking for help. At the end of the school year, as the school plans classes for the following September, teachers are keen to get students who have had our program because they cooperate and help one another. This anecdotal evidence of an increase in cooperation has been strongly borne out by research on the Roots of Empathy program.

The baby becomes a laboratory for human development—the development of a whole person, physical, social, emotional, intellectual, moral and spiritual. Students are coached in learning how to reflect. Every child is encouraged to speak out in the group, to find their voice, and to anchor the feeling of being a contributing member of a group in which there are no wrong answers or stupid questions, and respect is guaranteed.

Although I began the program with kindergarten children, by the end of my first year I was getting requests from teachers to expand into higher grades. There was a strong sense that through the Roots of Empathy program children were developing levels of emotional literacy that not only encouraged a healthy sense of self but contributed to a kinder, more respectful tone in the group. The program was also sought after for Grade 8 classes; in communities where schools were experiencing drop-outs due to adolescent pregnancies, the teachers and principals felt that understanding the emotional and physical needs of babies and the long reach that the first year has in a child's life would be very important for these young students. I reworked the curriculum to address the social and emotional learning that is relevant for this age group. By offering these teens experience with a baby, we help them to understand that every baby is entitled to have parents who can provide her with the best possible life. More than that, we give them a way to reflect on the realities of the upheaval that would result in their own lives if they became parents before they were ready. The concept of giving adolescents realistic insight into parenting, with many opportunities for dialogue with parents "in the trenches" and reflection on the demands of caring for a baby, encourages young people to understand the hardship and long-lasting implications of teen pregnancy. In one Grade 8 class our parent was a pediatrician. A student asked if it was fun being a parent. The mom replied, "In a twenty-four-hour day, there are fifteen minutes of pure joy and twenty-three hours and forty-five minutes of hard work."

By involving children in the unfolding story of the parent–child relationship, Roots of Empathy is engaging them in a world of social and emotional learning that examines the development of a human being on a green blanket on the classroom floor. This program addresses children's affective side, their ability to care. Empathy is a key ingredient of competent parenting, and exploration of what it takes to be a responsive and responsible parent opens the door to emotional literacy for children, creating change from the inside out. The skills they learn in the program will not only help them with relationships today but will affect the quality of parenting we can expect in the next generation. These skills will help children develop the empathy, insights and capacity for human connection that are critical for them to take their place in the world.

The Birth of Roots of Empathy

Where did the idea of offering such a program to elementary school children come from? Why was the curriculum built around the concept of bringing a baby into the classroom? What impact for families and society did I envision? The answers to these questions takes me back to my first years as an elementary teacher.

When I took my first teaching job, it was with hope and determination to make a difference in children's lives. I was so excited about teaching—which was perhaps surprising, since my sister and I used to pray in our early teens to be spared the dreaded fate of a "calling" to be a nun or a teacher. Although as two girls in convent school we hoped to avoid the vocation, as adults we both chose to teach, my sister moving on to teach children music while I chose kindergarten.

I thought I could make the world perfect for my students. Instead, I found myself face to face with the reality of little children's lives. Seeing those three-, four- and five-year-olds come into the classroom on the first day changed my whole perception. You could tell, right from that initial entrance, which ones were going to be winners, and which ones would struggle. The kind of start they had had in life determined their overall sense of competence and their ability to cope with the stress of transition to school. Some children came into the room with "SUCCESS" stamped on their foreheads. Even the ones who were a little shy, or upset at being separated from their parents, had an air of confidence, of knowing they were valued. They were ready to learn and participate in the group life of the school. As the weeks went by, they demonstrated that readiness in the classroom.

Other children came in warily, or bristling with aggression. Already the experiences of their first few years of life had taught them that their needs didn't matter, that adults couldn't really be trusted, that they'd better keep an eye out for threats all the time. The damage of neglect was as profound as the damage of abuse. Right from their first day of school, these children were swimming upstream. They wore their wounds in their behaviour. Learning was hard for them. Getting along with their classmates was a challenge. The school was not ready for them, but had confirmed the negative messages they'd been given from birth and their lack of school-readiness.

I began to see that if I was to truly make a difference for children, I would need to take a step back. Kindergarten was too late.

One thing all the children had in common was that they all loved their parents and were fiercely loyal to them. This was true whether their home was filled with privilege and harmony or beset with hardship and conflict. So I called the parents, and said to them, "If you'll share with me what you know about your children, I'll share with you what I know about preparing them for success in school." In all the work I have done with parents and children in the ensuing thirty years, what I had glimpsed darkly as a young teacher has become crystal clear: the relationship between the child and the parent is the most powerful teaching relationship there is. The home has a profound impact on the child's attitude to learning and their sense of competence before they even start school. Parents are children's most important teachers. It is the experiences of the early years, mediated by parenting, that set the child on a trajectory for either success or failure. A child's confidence, her concept of self, her readiness to launch herself into fearless learning and healthy relationships is dependent on and intricately bound up in the quality of nurturing she receives from a loving adult.

Building on these insights, I spent the next twenty-five years working with parents and their preschool children creating and refining programs that sustain and enrich the potential of the parent-child relationship. (The story of the Parenting and Family Literacy Centres which I developed to house these programs is told in Appendix A, see page 229) The programs were based on a premise of respect and empathy for parents and a belief that they want to do their best for their children. Parents were supported in discovering the ways that little children learn: through love and encouragement, emotional connection, authentic conversations and meaningful play. The power of parenting to positively affect children's success is well documented. The "Early Years Study" prepared for the Ontario government by Dr. Fraser Mustard and the Honourable Margaret Norrie McCain makes a powerful statement about this connection: "It is clear that the early years from conception to age six have the most important influence of any time in the life cycle on brain development and subsequent learning, behaviour and health. The effects of early experience, particularly during the first three years, on the wiring and sculpting of the brain's billions of neurons, last a lifetime."[2]

While I remain involved in training professionals in the parenting field, I no longer run these programs. I do, however, take every opportunity to visit them and introduce them to others interested in starting up parenting initiatives. The programs remain vibrant, encouraging parents to be their children's teachers and cheerleaders, creating the architecture for lifelong learning.

I like to express the scientific reality behind parenting programs in three words: love grows brains. The three requirements for optimal brain development are good nutrition, good nurturance and good stimulation. A newborn's brain has billions of neurons, but the pathways connecting those neurons are largely undeveloped. It is the experiences that a baby has in the first months and years that will "wire" the brain and prepare him for future learning. It is vital that the baby's needs are met in the context of a healthy and loving parent–child relationship.

The First Roots of Empathy Program

My years of working with young parents, many of them scarcely beyond childhood themselves, led me to wonder if one is ever too young to learn what makes a good parent, to realize what a baby needs to get a good start in life. It was a teen mother who jolted me into the transformative moment that crystallized my thinking about the need to break the intergenerational transmission of violence and negative patterns of parenting. Amy hadn't shown up to the Monday parenting program, so I went to visit her on my way home. She had been beaten yet again by her boyfriend, who had smashed her in the eye resulting in stitches across the eyelid and eyebrow. This boyfriend was also her pimp and was attempting to get her addicted to crack so that she would sell herself more willingly. She explained that she didn't want to come to the program because the other teen mothers would tell her to leave him, and she said to me, "He's really sorry, he's never going to do it again, and he loves me." This moment was etched in my mind because I could see her little baby girl growing up to repeat the pattern of her mother's life. This young teen had been physically abused by her mother and sexually abused by her mother's various boyfriends. She had received little or no positive nurturing from her alcohol-addicted mother and was now craving affection and attention in any way she could get it, even at the risk of violence to herself and her child. The challenge was to prevent her little daughter from following in her mother's footsteps; the challenge was to find a way out of repeating the cycle of addiction, violence, low literacy and poor parenting that was being passed on from one generation to the next.

Just as empathy lay at the heart of the parenting programs, it was also clearly the foundation of a program that could reach children and offer them not just a window on nurturing, responsive parenting, but an entire spectrum of social and emotional learning. It was clear to me that there was not enough room in the school curriculum to give these essential aspects of empathic human development the attention they deserved. More than that, I daily witnessed how learning was compromised as children's energies were depleted through the challenges of becoming part of the social group in the classroom or through coping with social aggression in the schoolyard. I visualized an approach that would strengthen the ability of children to build a solid sense of self-worth and caring relationships with others, a concrete program that would help them create an image of themselves as people who could make a difference in the world.

In 1996, Maytree Foundation[3] funded the conceptual development and implementation of a pilot Roots of Empathy program. The pilot was launched in kindergarten classrooms. An enthusiastic principal and a nucleus of compassionate teachers, familiar with the successes being experienced by children and parents in the parenting programs, opened their doors and worked with me through the evolution of the first year. There was a clear logic to parenting programs for parents—they have an immediate need and a strong interest in interacting with and learning about their children's development. But what were the features about learning to be a parent that would catch the imagination of children and enrich their experience of the world? For them, the years when they would be responsible for a baby seemed far away. What would make it real for them? In the original parenting programs, the learning for preschoolers was solidly experiential— activities were designed to allow them to see and touch and feel, to connect the concrete with the concept. As I started to apply the principles of experience-based learning to building concepts of responsive parenting in programs for school-aged children, it was clear that the concrete "learning tools" had to be the relationship between a parent and baby. I engaged and trained the people I knew to be the most knowledgeable about and committed to the value of the parent–child relationship. They were the parenting workers I had worked with for many years and they stood with me through the first year as I built, lesson by lesson, the themes that became the Roots of Empathy program.

Once I had the idea to bring a real baby and parent into the classroom, giving children the opportunity to observe the baby's development and the interaction between the baby and the parents over a school year, I could see the enormous scope for revealing how this relationship becomes the venue for developing social and emotional competence. Thinking through the dynamics of interaction in such a program, I realized that the learning would flow from the baby, that the baby would be the teacher. Over the years, I had witnessed countless times the impact a baby makes on the people around him. In the realms of emotional response and trust, a baby has no "agenda." He comes predisposed to love and expect the best from everyone in his sphere; he has no inhibitions or wiles to disguise how he is feeling and what he needs. He is a pure representation of what it is to be human and how to interact empathically with other humans. He is where the roots of empathy begin. In the early parenting programs that were part of the public school system in Toronto, we often had visits from older children in the regular classrooms who were having a rough day or acting out in class. They were permitted to visit us because it had a calming effect for them. The calming effect was the baby. There were always babies in the centre to create a flow of warmth and receptivity for each child—the frustrations and chaos of feelings that were too prickly to address head-on could be talked about through interacting with the baby.

Roots of Empathy is a program with many layers. It offers an experiential insight into competent parenting: understanding how a baby communicates, learning issues of infant safety and infant development. But it takes the learning that occurs with the baby in the classroom and builds it into a broader exploration of how humans understand and value themselves and each other. This vision was born of my conviction that babies were the perfect way to explore all that is valuable in the human experience, all that is critical in building healthy relationships, all that is indispensable in creating strong communities and a civil society. This program could teach a literacy of feeling. Through observation of the baby's emotions, children could learn about their own emotions and the emotions of others, learn to take the perspective of another, understand the power for resolving conflict that lies in being able to see a situation and the world from another person's viewpoint. I was convinced that the transformative potential of such a program was enormous. I had no doubt that it had the power to increase the emotional competence, the collaborative skills and the parenting capacity of a whole generation, child by child, classroom by classroom, community by community.

Many initiatives have been tried in schools to give children exposure to the role of being a parent. Children are given a plastic doll to care for, or eggs that they have to carry with them and look after. The aim of such programs is to recreate or imitate aspects of the parenting experience. What Roots of Empathy does is give children the experience *directly*, including interaction with a real baby in that baby's first year of life. Our program goes deeper still—as I cannot say too often—in that it fosters the development of empathy in the students, and this is a core component of successful parenting.

All babies are powerful teachers. One of our instructors said that her first meeting with the Grade 7/8 class to which she was assigned was very intimidating and the class was quite unruly. She was nervous about the family visit, especially because one of the boys, who was coping with behavioural challenges, had said he would tell the baby that he was ugly and stupid. As soon as the mother and baby walked through the door, though, the students were mesmerized and participated positively and enthusiastically. In fact, the boy who had spoken so negatively at the earlier session was, at the end of the class, the first one to head over to the baby and ask if he could hold him. And the mother who brought her baby to that first class could hardly wait to come back the following month to show how he had grown and the new skills he had learned.

Choosing a Roots of Empathy Baby

When we work with a community interested in bringing a Roots of Empathy program to their local school, those included in the planning are not just school board staff and parents; public health nurses, youth workers or volunteers from local service organizations often play a role. These are the people who are involved in and know the community; they know which family has just welcomed a new arrival. Our advice on recruiting a Roots of Empathy family is geared towards ensuring the richest experience for the students. This means finding parents who are enthusiastic about what Roots of Empathy offers to children, are willing to share with them the important first year of their baby's life, and can commit to a regular schedule of classroom visits. We look for families who live in the school neighbourhood, and who represent its diversity. We are not looking for "super babies" or "Gucci moms." Borrowing from Bruno Bettelheim, I say, "We are looking for the 'good-enough parent.'"[4]

Roots of Empathy babies are between two and four months old at the beginning of the program. Bringing the baby into the classroom as early in his life as possible allows for a greater range of infant development stages over the year and optimizes the learning opportunities for the students. Our emphasis on bringing a baby from the school's neighbourhood has the added benefit of connecting a new family with the school. This helps to strengthen the sense of community between families and schools and also makes it more likely that the Roots of Empathy family reflects the cultural makeup of the school. When babies are from one of a number of a school's cultural groups, the good feelings and connections that develop between the children and "their" baby inevitably spill over into a stronger sense of inclusiveness within the community. We encourage families where the father can come for visits as well as, or instead of, the mother; this can provide a sorely needed perspective in classrooms where children have little or no experience with a male in a nurturing role. We have had single parent families both mother-led and, occasionally, father-led.

In one of our kindergarten classes, baby Tama visited each month with his mother, and on a number of occasions his father was able to join them. Their reflections on the experience reveal the exchange of learning that occurred. Tama's mother, Theresa, who is of Maori heritage, sang Maori lullabies in the classroom and was impressed with the intense involvement of children who were five years old. She commented that "The children were genuinely interested in what Tama could or could not achieve so it was very easy to answer their questions. We were surprised at the maturity the children displayed and the words they became used to using—like *temperament, transition, milestones* and *communication*. Some of the children found the words difficult to say but they clearly understood what they meant." Tama's parents, as so many parents in our program do, commented on how much the interactions in the classroom taught them about children.

Branching Out

Roots of Empathy has grown exponentially. It is offered in schools across Canada and Australia. We have reached almost 29,000 students so far in 2005. The news spreads from community to community—by word of mouth, through media coverage and through educators sharing best practices. When a community hears there's a school-based program out there that involves a local family, makes a positive difference in how children treat each other today and prepares them to be good citizens and good parents in the future, Roots of Empathy is invited in. Members of our staff then collaborate with the community to build a committed group of people who champion the program, choose potential instructors and work with the schools to get the program up and running.

Globalization has made the world a much smaller place and heightened the commonality of the issues we struggle with. We are plagued with conflict and violence in schools. Our program offers practical hope. We are at a time and a place where a new way forward is sorely needed. Through the eyes of a baby, Roots of Empathy takes us back to the basics of what it is to be truly human.

Roots of Empathy in Our World

I invite every parent, every educator, every individual concerned with shaping the next generation to examine the learnings culled from the parent–baby relationship. The chapters in this book are presented to you as windows into the world of Roots of Empathy. They are designed to reveal to you the layers of learning experienced by children in the classroom and reveal the wisdom of children's responses to those experiences.

Parents will draw from Roots of Empathy an affirmation of the fundamental influence they have on their children from the first breath and even in utero. The dance of intimacy, conducted through glances, smiles, rocking and soothing words gives infants a secure base from which to successfully engage the world—from forming healthy relationships to exploring their physical space, tackling problems and learning how to learn. In the holistic environment of this program, we name, describe and give life to concepts in neuroscience and child development. Parents will recognize in these lessons that what they do instinctively is critical to raising a generation of children who have the skills and emotional competence to create a more civil society. Through Roots of Empathy, we can break the cycle of passing on damaging behaviours, whether these be violent or neglectful or unempathic, from one generation to the next.

Educators—teachers, school administrators—in many, many school settings across Canada have witnessed what this program adds to the dynamics of the classroom, to the life of the school and to the learning of individual children. By witnessing the development of a baby over the course of a year in the context of the parenting relationship, the program ensures a solid foundation in social and emotional learning. Communication skills, through discussion, art, writing and music, are an important component of every class we offer. An elementary school vice-principal told me, "I get so excited about all of the curriculum connections—I know if I were the classroom teacher with this opportunity, my whole program would revolve around Roots of Empathy." An additional compelling feature of having this program in schools is the strong body of evidence that links the development of empathic skills with academic success. When empathy training is integrated into the classroom, critical thinking skills, reading comprehension and creative thinking are enhanced.[5]

Many observers and participants who have witnessed the unfolding of Roots of Empathy in a classroom over the course of a year have suggested that it is nothing short of revolutionary in its potential to change the way young people see themselves and their world. Change-makers directly involved in social policy development, whose vocation it is to find ways to address the ills that plague our society, be it domestic abuse, child abuse, bullying in schools, the devastating effects of FASD (fetal alcohol spectrum disorder) or youth violence, will find support in this program. Every tenet of the program is aimed at inculcating respect for oneself, understanding and compassion for others, and a sense of responsibility for the world, its citizens and its future. In this respect, it is a powerful preventative program aimed at addressing those very ills that policy-makers are concerned with. Key longitudinal studies done in the United States show that the cost of prevention in children's early years is a fraction of the cost of responding to the needs of individuals when they fall off the rails and become involved with social services and the judicial system.[6] Justice Edward Ormston, a criminal court judge, once told me, "If the lessons that children learn in Roots of Empathy could have been taught to the people I deal with every day, we'd have far less need for prisons." Justice Ormston is now a member of our board.

The way we treat and care for children has an indelible impact on our school system, our economy and our future. We cannot afford to underestimate the critical role of empathy in moral development and our motivation for justice.[7] Nor can we afford to underestimate the importance of the early years and the family in building the kind of world where full participation of every citizen is a given, where we breathe peace and social justice and where empathy is in the water supply. Roots of Empathy shows how an infant can lead the way.

2

EMPATHY:
WHAT IT IS AND
WHY IT MATTERS

I am proud when I
make new friends

What Is Empathy?

IN ONE GRADE 4 CLASS, nine-year-old Sylvie was wearing running shoes that did up with a Velcro strap. Some of the other children taunted her, saying she wore "baby shoes" and "geeky shoes." She was the target of a double-barrelled criticism—her shoes were not only cheap and unfashionable, they were immature. This is the kind of humiliation that would shrivel the spirit of any nine-year-old. But then something happened. When the class headed outside for recess, Sylvie's best friend June

swapped one shoe with her. The empathic insight and quick thinking of that child gives us hope. Her actions said, "I'm your friend
and I'm proud to wear your shoes and be just like you." She turned
a mean, exclusionary attack into something playful, without saying a word. Every other child in the class got the message: "This is
my friend, make fun of her and you are making fun of me. Keep it
up and you may find yourself outnumbered by kids who care."

In his paper "Truth and Ethics in School Reform," the philosopher Thomas McCollough writes, "Moral imagination is the capacity to empathize with others, i.e., not just to feel for oneself, but to
feel with and for others. This is something that education ought
to cultivate and that citizens ought to bring to politics." [1] Empathy is frequently defined as the ability to identify with the feelings
and perspectives of others. I would add *and to respond appropriately*
to the feelings and perspectives of others. Expressed this way, it
sounds simple enough. Perhaps it is only when we reflect on what
happens when empathy is absent that we begin to grasp the profound, complex and fundamental role it plays in the healthy functioning of human relations.

When we think of the Holocaust or South Africa under apar-
theid we are horrified at the scale of cruelty perpetrated on an
entire race of people. We might try to distance ourselves from
the injustice by focusing on the fact it was long ago or far away and
couldn't happen here, couldn't happen now. But think it through.
Were the people who participated in these affronts to human
rights, or stood by and watched them happen, fundamentally
different from us? And if they weren't, what force was at work
that drew them into a situation that we find unconscionable? In
both cases, a tremendous amount of propaganda, indoctrination
and intimidation went into convincing the dominant population
that Jews, that black South Africans, were alien, threatening or
something less than human. But we know that while a great many

people were either active or passive participants, many others resisted the propaganda and actively involved themselves in helping victims and struggling for change. It is crucial to understand what accounts for the difference in these two kinds of responses. The difference lies in our capacity for empathy, our ability to identify with the feelings and perspectives of others. If we cannot see the other person as human like us, we will not be able to identify with him. If we cannot put ourselves in his place, we will not recognize his experiences and feel what he feels. This failure of empathy at best leads to complicity and apathy; at worst, it leads to cruelty and violence. We could learn a lot from the nine-year-old girl with the Velcro shoe. She stood up to injustice and confronted cruelty and unfairness where she found it.

On a less historical, global scale, the same forces are at work in the bullying that plagues our schools and communities. The victim is singled out on a number of grounds—perhaps because she is smaller, weaker, has poor social skills and few friends, or is a new immigrant, talks differently, has a different skin colour. Whatever the factors, they are used to marginalize the victim, to define her as different and inferior to the dominant group. She then becomes not only the victim of the bully, but also—to a lesser, but still hurtful, degree—the victim of the onlookers. The research on bullying confirms that a strong characteristic of the bully is a lack of empathy. In the case of onlookers, fear of or admiration for the bully outweighs their ability to feel or act on empathy for the victim. The consequences for everyone are severe: a toxic environment is created in which the bullying behaviour is not challenged, and children are not given the skills and confidence to stand up to the bully, to stand up for themselves and to stand up in defence of the victim. When we do not actively work to turn this around, we are failing to give our children the tools to form healthy, respectful relationships. We are failing to show them that bullying is destructive and we are failing to give them a sense of their role as members of a civil society.

An extreme outcome of this failure can be seen in the case of Reena Virk, the fourteen-year-old British Columbia schoolgirl who died following a brutal beating by her peers. There were eight teens, seven of them girls, directly involved in the beating. Other boys and girls watched it happen and only one witness made any attempt to intervene. No one reported the attack until Reena had been missing for four days. One of the girls involved has recently been convicted of second-degree murder in Reena's death following a third trial. At the trial, evidence was given that Reena was kicked in the head, that attempts were made to set her hair on fire and that she was held under water until she stopped moving. Among the lessons we have to learn from this tragedy is that physical bullying has been "degendered"—it can no longer be seen as the purview of the male throwing his weight around. Just as critical is the fact that most of these young people were fourteen years old. It is obvious that, if we are going to change the conditions that allow such things to happen, we have to work with children from a much earlier age.

Nature is on our side in creating strong, empathic societies. We are born with the capacity for empathy. An ability to recognize emotions transcends race, culture, nationality, social class and age. Researchers have shown photographs of human faces to people of various ages around the world. Without hesitation, the people can point out which photo shows someone who is afraid, someone who is happy, someone who is worried, someone who is sad. Our feelings, and our expression of them, are universal.[2] Show a tribal chieftain in Mali a photo of a little Japanese girl who is frightened, and he will immediately be able to recognize how she is feeling—despite the differences in race, clothing and culture. The emotions, and their expression, are the same. Clearly, our emotions and the need to have them understood by others are so basic that the visible signals of how we are feeling have become essential aspects of humans around the world.

This is our deepest connection with one another. Roots of Empathy stretches children to find points of intersection. In their discussions about being sad, children may give reasons for sadness that are different—"My parents fight a lot" or "Kids make fun of me because I have two moms instead of a mom and a dad"—but there is understanding about the feeling itself, and that shared understanding creates channels of connection and belonging that lead to empathy.

Babies and toddlers will spontaneously respond to the sadness or happiness of their mother or other significant people in their lives. They are attuned to nuances of harmony or discordance. This capacity for empathy grows as the child develops a sense of self, separate from other people. The more aware the child becomes of his own emotions and their effect on him, the more he is capable of recognizing emotional states in people around him and aware of the effects created by different emotions. An eighteen-month-old will respond to the distress of another child by giving him a toy or bringing an adult over to help.[3] This is the beginning of developing a moral sense and a capacity for pro-social behaviour. These stages in the development of empathy—awareness of self, understanding of emotions, ability to attribute emotions to others and take the perspective of the other person—are critical for positive socialization.[4]

From the outset, parents are the single most important influence on how a child's innate capacity for empathy grows and develops. It is this first relationship that affirms the power and efficacy of human connection: Baby is hungry and starts to cry, Mommy listens and cues into Baby's hunger, Mommy picks Baby up, comforts him and feeds him. Daddy smiles, sings Baby's name, lifts her in the air; Baby has an answering smile, gurgles, spreads out her fingers to touch Daddy's face. Circles of communication, understanding and connection are completed. These and similar circles are repeated throughout the first years of life. The give-and-take of reading cues and responding to cues lays the foundation for the emotional learning that allows empathy to take root and flourish.

Home is where the start is; it is where children become themselves; it is where, before the age of six, their values and attitudes are formed. The roots of empathy, laid down in the home, give children the foundation, the confidence, the strong sense of self to build relationships in the bigger world outside the home. The familiar patterns they have learned form the template for reading and responding to the behaviours and emotional expression of other children and adults. The approach to communication, caring and sorting out problems that is built into the emotional ebb and flow of family life can lead to understanding the benefits of sharing and forming friendships in the sandbox, in the schoolhouse and in the boardroom. What more valuable support can we as a society provide to children and their parents than to ensure that this early social and emotional learning, so critical to successful relationships in life is a part of our child-care and education structures? What would add more to our progress as a global society than to place at least as much value on the development of positive, fully realized human relationships as we place on the acquisition of academic skills? What greater contribution could we make to our sustainable future than to promote a development of the heart that runs parallel to the development of the mind?

Why Empathy Matters

One of the parents of a child in a Roots of Empathy class called the teacher and said, "I don't know what you are doing in that class, but Cody has completely changed the way he treats his baby brother. He is gentle, protective and very loving." Cody has taken to heart what he has been learning about empathy and the needs of babies in the context of the classroom and transferred it to his home situation. This parent's story is, happily, very common.

We also frequently see the healing power of empathy. Liam, who was expressing a lot of anger and frustration in his class at the beginning of the program, gradually responded to the smiles and overtures the baby frequently directed at him and formed a strong, positive connection with her. Over the course of a few visits, the baby seemed to actively favour connection with Liam, slowly drawing him to her, and the instructor felt Liam turned a corner the day he looked at the baby and the baby smiled at him. At the end of that session, Liam touched the baby's feet to say goodbye. This was an "opening up" that led to the child, for the first time that year, establishing eye contact with others and beginning to interact positively with his classmates. I have observed this "wise baby syndrome" in countless classes. The baby has an intuitive sense of who needs her, an uncanny knack of zeroing in on the child who is unpopular, carrying a burden of pain, uncommunicative, struggling in some way. The baby sees the child, this other human being, purely and without judgment. The child sees his best true self reflected back by the baby's response and, with it, the opportunity to reinvent himself.

These are just two examples of the power of empathy to re-shape relationships. Understanding how other people feel is the first step to building caring relationships in the classroom, in the community and in the world at large. In our program the babies teach this lesson for us, because they express their feelings in such a clear, open way. The baby who is happy is happy with every cell of his body. The baby who is frightened is the epitome of fear, and this is easy for children to recognize. The observation of emotions in the baby is the gateway that leads the children to identify and label their own emotions and is a curriculum bridge to learning to recognize emotions in others. In one of the exercises in class the students look at illustrations of children their own age and talk about how the people in the pictures are feeling. The concrete experience with the baby stimulates a thoughtful range of responses. Talking about what they are learning from the baby's cues gives children the language and experience of talking out loud about feelings; it gives them permission to have a public discourse about emotions and the process of talking fine-tunes their thinking.

Social skills are built on empathy and emotional intelligence: when you understand your own feelings and can recognize those of others, you are able to reach out and make connections. That means giving comfort and solace to those who are hurt, and celebrating with those who are happy. If we could be more present and responsive to each other, we wouldn't have so many people running on empty. In the Roots of Empathy classroom we encourage the building of friendships, giving children the experience of making connections through shared feelings. When we do the classroom activity in which children look at a picture of a sad girl and talk not only about why she might be sad but also about how they could help her, they often attribute her sadness to loneliness and a lack of friends. The solutions invariably include taking steps to bring the girl into their circle of friends. While they may not often articulate it, children intuitively know that friendship mitigates pain and bolsters us against the emotional landmines of growing up. Through this building of empathy and emotional awareness we have an opportunity to improve the interactions of children today and affect the quality of human interaction in the next generation.

When I talk about some of my experiences with Roots of Empathy classes, and describe some of the touching incidents when children demonstrate their courage and compassion, people in the audience are often moved to tears. Many are embarrassed by this—I see them trying to wipe their eyes discreetly with tissues concealed in their hands. Why should we be embarrassed? Those tears are proof that we are human—that we feel.

We need to make a healthy place for emotions in the way we perceive ourselves and in the way we deal with each other, regardless of gender or how old we are.

Empathy, Literacy of the Emotions

In our program, we give all the children the words to describe their feelings. Focusing on the core emotions, we ask them to tell us about times when they felt sad, scared, angry or happy. Listening to the other children and sharing their own story enlarges their vocabulary and sparks the recognition that is an essential part of emotional intelligence: "I hear how you are feeling, and I know I have felt the same way. We are alike." When we have given shape to the solidarity of humankind it will no longer be possible for us to hive off a group and dehumanize them.

Studies tell us that when girls have a problem, they typically talk about it with others. When boys have a problem, often, their response is to act, to *do* something. It is still a facet of our culture that boys are not often encouraged to talk about their feelings and consequently lack the vocabulary to express emotion. Nurturing an ease in reading and expressing emotion in boys is particularly important. It is still true that parents talk more to girls than they do to boys, and that girls usually have a larger emotional vocabulary than boys. Our experience has found that boys who have gone through the Roots of Empathy program have a vocabulary of feeling words as large as that of the girls, and are more likely to talk about problems and emotions than the boys who have not had this experience. This is possible through the great care taken to make the classroom a safe place of trust.

Beyond having the language to discuss emotions, children need to know their feelings are accepted and valued by the adults around them. When you respect children's feelings, they learn to respect the feelings of others. When our babies are frightened, we cuddle and comfort and reassure them. The message the baby gets is that his fear is acknowledged and responded to. When older children are frightened—especially if those children are boys— we tend to dismiss their fears and sometimes impart a sense of shame or imply weakness. In contrast to the loving acknowledgment they received as babies, they are now getting an entirely different message: their emotions are not acceptable and it is better to suppress them. Every time we don't see or hear or respond to a child's emotional expression, we are depriving that child of emotional oxygen. By the time most of us are adults, we are not willing to admit to fear, even to ourselves. We will make ourselves ill rather than become vulnerable emotionally by acknowledging feelings that we define as weak.

We even shroud our positive emotions. Why do we consider it inappropriate for an adult to show unbridled joy when we so prize its spontaneous, unguarded expression in children? If we cannot show fear or sadness, and can't display our happiness, what is left for us to feel? No wonder so many adults explode in anger or collapse with depression. But we see these effects in children, too. With rapidly escalating rates of childhood depression, it is more critical than ever that we give our children the tools to express their emotions in a safe and healthy way and that we, as adults, give our children the strongest sense of their right to be heard and understood. It is equally critical that we teach them to do the same for others. A remarkable instance of healthy emotional expression emerged from a Grade 7 classroom discussion of "transitional objects," the soothing blanket or toy that helps a baby go to sleep. The instructor was amazed as Grade 7 boys talked of special toys from babyhood that they still had in their rooms at home. Delighted at the ease of the unfolding conversation, she said later, "It was surprising they felt so comfortable sharing this because they do have a certain image to protect!"

Knowledge may influence decision-making, but it is emotion that truly changes behaviour. How many people know they should be eating better and exercising more? They've heard the message from their doctors, seen the warnings on television, and yet they continue to eat junk food and spend long hours on the couch. They have the knowledge, but their emotions are not engaged. When a person does change his eating or activity level, it is usually because of some emotional event: the fear generated by a heart attack or the desire to be more physically attractive to the opposite sex after a divorce. Children exert a strong emotional pull in influencing social change and people will do many things out of love for their children that they would not do for other reasons. Think of wearing seat belts or bicycle helmets, quitting smoking or refusing to drink and drive. It is no accident that children appear so often in advertising, whether the product is cereal or cars. Emotion, not information, makes the difference. We tend to undervalue the role of emotion in our lives and see being emotional as a fault.

Empathy also has an important role to play in fostering interdependence. Interdependence is critical at all levels of our lives— at work, at home, in our community relationships. The idea that independence represents strength and interdependence is a weak distant cousin is deeply flawed. Studies of cultures that place a high value on independence show that the success of the individual is prized more than collaborative achievements. By contrast, in cultures where there is an interdependence of roles and responsibilities among extended family and within the community, where children have a contribution to make to the subsistence of their family, a high value is placed on altruistic behaviour and working for the common good.[5] A recent tragic incident in

Toronto involved the death of a five-year-old boy who fell from a high-rise balcony. It was ten o'clock at night and his mother had just left her son in the care of two older siblings (nine and eleven years old) to go to work. Amid the gasps of outrage about a mother who would leave such a young child without adequate supervision there were some compassionate voices asking, "Where was her support system? Why was she put in the position of having to leave her children so she could put food on the table?" For this woman, a recent immigrant who had lost both her husband and her mother and who had no support network to rely on, the cost of struggling alone was tragically high.[6] A caring society, in which empathy was a core value, would have had answers for her. There would have been people who felt it their duty as members of the community to intervene compassionately when her children needed supervision or help. There is great strength in the closeness of the connections we build through interdependence, and this is ultimately the strength of a community. A community of completely independent people is not a community at all.

A Child Is a Person

Our approach to children is not working, and the consequences for all of us are huge. It is clear that inaccurate and inadequate information about the needs of children continues to undermine our efforts. To oversimplify, despite all the new knowledge we have about children's cognitive and emotional development, a theory of childhood that remains all too pervasive in our society is that children are in many ways less than fully human. This theory sees children's emotions, for example, as being unimportant. A baby cries, and the parents are warned, "He's just spoiled. Leave him to cry." A little seven-year-old boy is frightened by a barking dog and someone is sure to say, "Big boys don't cry. There's nothing to be scared of." We are a child-illiterate society. We have begun to have legislation that recognizes the unique needs of disabled citizens but have not yet to plan for the unique needs of our youngest citizens. Children are seen as nuisances and are unwanted in many public buildings, public spaces and some apartment buildings.

We replace an understanding of real, individual children with clichés. That all children lead lives of happy innocence, without worry or responsibility, is a common cliché that can have tragic consequences. By failing to see that a child's range and depth of emotion can be as complex as our own, we allow ourselves to ignore the signs of stress or depression in the troubled children around us. In Roots of Empathy classrooms we have ample evidence that even when children do not have well-developed intellectual abilities, their range of emotional expression can be rich and fully developed. We may tell ourselves that the child who is crying is not really distressed and cannot have a good reason for his tears, or that the child who is imitating the violence she experiences at home by fighting with her classmates is just misbehaving and deserves punishment. But if we do, we are throwing a blanket over a child's emotions and there will be a price to pay.

There are still adults who subscribe to the theory that children are naturally cruel and self-centred. That belief ignores the many examples of children who demonstrate a thoughtfulness and kindness that often surpasses that of adults. In a Roots of Empathy class that included a nine-year-old boy in a wheelchair who drooled uncontrollably, we saw how brilliantly children can advocate for the human rights of a classmate. Children in this class explained to the other children in the school how their friend felt when others made fun of him. All name-calling stopped. I believe also that adults must always take responsibility and must always intervene when bullying occurs, not just to protect the victims but to give the bullies and the onlookers the support they need to act differently. That belief is supported by a substantial body of research, indicating that a bullying environment takes stronger hold when adults do not intervene to protect the victims and deal with the bullying behaviour.[7]

Children know this. In a Grade 5 / 6 class, the instructor introduced the topic of bullying and how to end it. When one student suggested that you could "teach the bully a lesson" by doing to the bully whatever he had done to the victim, another student immediately said, "But then wouldn't you become the bully?" Other voices joined in, strategies were discussed, and the student consensus was: "Bullying is never justified. Believe in yourself. Trust your friends. Ask an adult for help." The children's solution illuminates their understanding that everyone is involved in putting a stop to bullying.

With a little support from us, children reveal depths of understanding and social genius that will astound us.

Empathy Is Caught Not Taught

Our program seeks to build a classroom environment where strength arises out of connection and respectful relationships, a classroom environment where, as children build those relationships, they learn how they are alike. Out of this arise skills in consensus-building, negotiating, empathy and self-awareness. Through the Roots of Empathy baby's first year of life, children are inhaling the social environment of relationship-building, not through dependence on instruction, but through the intrinsic learning experiences of a continuing connection. Values are communicated, and attitudes are internalized. The subtlest learning lies in what children catch from what they see and hear and from people's responses to them cumulatively, over time. We can only expect children to be empathic if they've had real and repeated experiences of empathy in their daily lives. Roots of Empathy opens a door to this world. For some children, who have ingested empathy with their breast milk, it is a familiar world; for other children, whose early circumstances have been less fortunate, it is a world they can feel welcome in and begin to own.

In our classrooms, each individual's emotions, preferences and opinions are important. No individual is more important than the other, and the goal is to find a way that everyone can feel validated—not the instructor at the expense of the child, or one child at the expense of another child, but everyone, each in a way that accords respect to that person.

One classroom teacher describes her Roots of Empathy children this way: "After a year of exposure to the program, I am amazed at their collective abilities to engage in critical thinking tasks. They are keen problem solvers, in small and large group settings. Individually, they are able to make independent decisions, no small achievement for six-year-olds! I have absolutely no bullying in my classroom, a feat I attribute solely to the program. In fact, my students have become self-appointed "peacemakers" on the playground, often bringing students from other grades and classes to our classroom to "solve the problem by talking it over."

When children are given the opportunity to take charge of their own problem-solving, they develop inner motivation and begin to find their way to becoming confident, contributing adults. They acquire a sense of pride that has nothing to do with vanity and everything to do with conviction. They don't do things so someone will like them or because they hope to get some recognition or another reward. They become true givers, because they have something extra to give. I believe that we will never get to altruism without empathy.

Empathy and the 3 R's

Debates on what constitutes a "good" education often pit the proponents of the "three R's" against those who place an emphasis on the need for schools to inculcate values. What is heartening to me is the growing body of thought that not only links these two positions but places empathy at the foundation of what is essential to academic success.

An empathic person has not only learned to understand the feelings, behaviour and intentions of others but also cares. Being able to communicate that understanding requires emotional literacy. The cognitive scientist B.F. Jones writes, "Successful students often recognize that much of their success involves their ability to communicate with others . . . they are also able to view themselves and the world through the eyes of others. This means . . . examining beliefs and circumstances of others, keeping in mind the goal of enhanced understanding and appreciation. . . . Successful students value sharing experiences with persons of different backgrounds as enriching their lives." [8]

A program that focuses on the development of empathy opens the doors of social and emotional learning for children, giving them skills of emotional perception that strengthen their sense of self and their ability to connect to and collaborate effectively with others throughout childhood and adolescence. This learning comes from emotion shared with classmates, attunement with the baby and communication with adults who are on the same emotional wavelength.

A school vice-principal who is also a Roots of Empathy instructor once shared just such a moment with me:

By the time of Jenna's second visit to the classroom, she was almost four months old and trying very hard to roll over. When we spoke about this in the post-family-visit class, the children found it awesome that a baby so small could be so determined, could put so much energy and concentration into this single accomplishment. They were particularly intrigued with what a little gymnast Jenna was as she grasped her feet and pulled them up. "She really, really wants to roll over—you can see it in her face and in her whole body!"

What was even more perceptive in this group of six- and seven-year-olds was the profound understanding of the concept of frustration. "It is so hard to want to do something really badly and just not be able to do it." There was general agreement on that. Then Daniel, with one of those insights that young children frequently show but which never fail to amaze the adults in their lives, said, "It must be so scary to not be able to control your own body." What an intuitive sense Daniel gave us of the complexity of emotions we experience when we are confronted with something new—the eagerness to make it happen, the thrill of discovery, and yet, the fear of not being in control.

The children were full of anticipation, awaiting Jenna's third visit. We had discussed their predictions about what she would be able to do by now and "rolling over" was a hot favourite. On the family-visit day, Jenna's mother placed her on her back on the green blanket. Almost immediately, she started twisting her body, stretching her arms, and swinging her feet off the floor and over to the side. Within seconds, she had flipped over onto her tummy and the class went wild. Every child was clapping and cheering. There was a community of delight that Jenna had reached a new milestone.

Daniel turned to Shakeel and said, "See, Shakeel, just like you. She can do it now." In the general excitement, no one asked Daniel what he meant. Later that morning, the children were drawing. Shakeel drew a picture of himself learning to ride his bike. "Just like Jenna," he said. Shakeel explained how difficult it was to learn to ride a two-wheeler. He had experienced lots of frustration. He was so glad that Daniel had been helping him after school and stuck with him till he was able to do it. Daniel had told him he deserved to succeed because he had worked so hard for so long to get it right.

It all clicked into place. Jenna's milestone, Shakeel's milestone. The children had transferred their insights in the classroom to their world outside the classroom. The vehicle was empathy.

This was a rich experience for everyone involved. Together, around their eagerness for the baby's achievement, they shared an emotion, established a strong sense of wishing others well and formed the kind of connection that binds people together and builds civil societies.

The immediate gains for children in the Roots of Empathy class are skills that enable them to be understood and to understand, and the critical blending of emotion, cognition and memory that will make them successful learners. And as future parents, they gain living experience of a model of competent parenting that they can bring to raising, caring for and teaching their own children. And, perhaps, most importantly of all, each of these advantages builds on the other to enrich our everyday interactions and creates the base for a society that values collaboration, interdependence and respects the voice of every member.

3

THE ROOTS OF EMPATHY CLASSROOM: MY TEACHER IS A BABY

Leah Teaches Class

WHILE WAITING for the children to return from playtime, Sharon, the Roots of Empathy instructor, is preparing the empty classroom for the expected baby visit. She opens a large tote bag and unfolds a bright green blanket. "This blanket defines the baby's space," she will explain. "The children will sit around it so they can all see the baby." She is careful to arrange it in the middle of the open space so that everyone will have enough room.

I introduced the idea of the blanket for several reasons: to create a germ-barrier between the students and the babies to reassure the nervous, first-time parents; to create a stage where all of the students can see the performance of life, the drama of growth and the miracle of attachment taking place; and to have a physical reminder for the younger children not to crawl over or run over and touch the baby impulsively. We set the children up for success when we establish rules and make it as easy as possible for them to comply. The blanket helps us do that.

Sharon takes one final glance in her bag at the toys she has selected to use during the lesson. The teacher arrives, and her students are not far behind. The toys, too, have been specially chosen for Roots of Empathy to be tools in demonstrating the baby's development, achievements and temperament. The baby plays differently with the toys during each visit and the children are able to observe the new skills he has developed. In fact, they chronicle the baby's development in many domains, they learn the baby's unique temperament, and notice the baby's feelings—is he frustrated? surprised? interested? determined?

Today's class is a kindergarten class, with all the energy and laughter you'd expect from a group of five-year-olds who have just been outside playing. They arrange themselves around the blanket, wriggling into their front-and-centre positions.

This is the age group where Roots of Empathy started. My idea was to begin with the youngest children and focus on developing a literacy of feelings that would help them navigate the rough waters of childhood. I believed that the pain and difficulty of not knowing how to identify or manage their emotions could be prevented if they had the tools for a rich social and emotional life, which they could use not just to build individual relationships but to take responsibility for creating a peaceful and compassionate classroom. I felt strongly that this was best launched at the earliest possible age. Before the age of two, children are already becoming aware of their own unique selves and of their emotions.[1] So it made a lot of sense to introduce the first program to a kindergarten class.

When six-month-old Leah and her mother appear in the doorway, there are murmurs of excitement around the room. "Let's sing our welcoming song," says Sharon, and leads them in singing.

As Leah's mother lifts her daughter out of the infant seat, all the children stand up and wait eagerly for Leah and her mother to walk around the circle. Each child smiles or says "Hi, Leah" or gently touches her foot in greeting. When Leah's mother puts her on the green blanket in a sitting position, the children gasp, "She's sitting, she's sitting." In their excitement they edge forward, calling Leah's name and waving to her. Malik points out: "Her mommy had to help her before and now she's sitting all by herself." Sharon tells the group, "This is called a milestone. Leah can do something she wasn't able to do before."

Then Sharon asks: "What do you think this means for Leah? What will be different in her life now that she can sit up?" There is a chorus of answers:

"She can see us better."
"She can point."
"She can reach for things."
"She can throw the ball to us now."
"She can hold an ice-cream."
Leah beams back at the smiling faces around her.
"Can she crawl yet?" asks a student.
"She's getting close to crawling," Leah's mother replies.

Sharon invites Leah's mom to lay Leah on her stomach. She wants the children to see for themselves. Other than waving her arms and kicking her feet, Leah can't move. "Her tummy is glued," says Tamara.

When Leah rolls over, the entire group buzzes with excitement. "She did that before. That was a milestone too, wasn't it?" says Jack.

When Leah begins to show distress, Sharon asks the class, "What is Leah telling us?'

There are several responses: "She wants her mommy." "She's mad." "She's tired." "She's frustrated."

"So what should we do?" asks Sharon.

"Give her to her mommy," the class says in unison.

Sharon has written a list on a flip chart showing some "baby milestones" such as crawling, sitting, walking. As Leah cuddles into her mommy's shoulder, Sharon reads them out and asks the children which of these things Leah can do now. They respond with a loud "Yes" to rolling over and sitting. When asked about crawling and walking, they say, in unison, "Not yet." For children this "not yet" is a very comforting reminder that they will eventually reach their own milestones. They may not be able to read a whole book yet but they can sound out a lot of words and that big milestone will come just as surely as Leah will learn to walk.

Sharon asks the class about how to keep Leah safe now that she can roll over and sit up. One child has a story to tell. When her mother was a baby, her grandmother left her for just a second on the change table, and the baby rolled right off onto the floor. The children nod in agreement when Sharon says babies shouldn't be left alone on a change table. Several children talk about how Leah can reach out and pull things down like a tablecloth, now that she can sit. There are lots of suggestions about the dangerous things that could be sitting on that tablecloth.

Leah's mother contributes, "When I leave her alone in a room, I put her in the playpen. And I'm getting safety gates for the stairways." She adds that she replaces Leah's pacifier every two or three months, because the rubber can wear out and become a choking hazard.

Leah begins to babble and the children laugh at the sounds she makes. When Sharon tries to get Leah's attention with a foot rattle, Leah rolls away from her and smiles at some of the children nearby. Sharon says, "I guess she's more interested in Reuben than the rattle!" The little boy sitting beside Reuben says, "No, she was smiling at me!" Reuben insists, "No, me!" Leah watches entranced as they argue good-naturedly for a minute, then Reuben concludes: "Okay, both of us." Sharon asks them how it feels when Leah smiles at them.

"Very happy. Smiley inside," they reply.

Sharon asks Leah's mother's permission to play "This Little Piggy" with Leah. When her mother agrees, she begins the song "This Little Piggy Went to Market." But after just two lines, Leah pulls her hand out of Sharon's hand and rolls over, closer to the children. She smiles up at them again. "What's Leah telling me now?" asks Sharon. "She doesn't want you to do 'Little Piggy,'" offers one child. "She wants to play with us," says another. They are adept at reading the baby's cues.

Gently, Sharon rolls Leah back into position and repeats the song "This Little Piggy" while holding each of Leah's fingers in turn. As she finishes, Leah pulls her hand away and begins to fuss. Her mother quickly picks her up, and Sharon comments: "Leah didn't like the piggy game but she's happy with her mommy." Sharon coaches the children through the social and emotional cues Leah used to solve her situation. "How did Leah tell her mommy that she needed her?"

"With her voice—she got whiny."

"What else did Leah do—what did she do with her hands?"

"She pulled her hands away from you."

"What about Leah's face? What did you see there?"

"She looked right at her Mommy with a grumpy face."

A wide yawn signals Leah has had enough. The time has passed quickly, but Leah and her mother are now ready to leave. When Sharon asks the students what they think should happen next, Malik and Tamara cry out, "It's time to sing the goodbye song."

The children sing their goodbye song as Leah's mother carries the baby around the perimeter of the blanket, stopping in front of each child. Some pat or squeeze Leah's feet, others hold her hand or just smile at her. One little boy stands up and hugs Leah's mother.

They continue to watch with interest as she puts Leah back in the car seat, tucking in the receiving blanket that Leah has been clutching. "Leah's a blanket girl," she says, explaining that Leah uses the blanket to comfort herself.

Why a Baby?

What is it about babies that makes them the most gifted teachers of empathy? A baby is the place we universally start from. In the classroom, the baby is both endearing and non-threatening, inviting into the circle of communication the most reticent, belligerent, disengaged and angry children. A baby and parent together form a powerful dyad that allows children to be present in an evolving drama starring the most influential, indelible and life-shaping relationship ever.

The baby and parent together on the green blanket in the Roots of Empathy classroom are a social science laboratory. We could watch a baby in isolation and catch something of the way she develops, how her temperament manifests itself, how she responds to her environment. But when we watch the symbiotic action—reaction of parent and child, the way the parent accommodates to the baby's energy level, to her mood, to her management of her environment, then we are witness to a human symphony. We are taken beyond the magic and charm of the baby and engaged in the life lesson of how we become responsive human beings when we are loved. The capacity to be human, to reach out and offer connection, develops through this first relationship of trust and unconditional love.

The children are invited to notice how the baby gauges his environment—is it safe? is it scary?—by constantly checking his mother's face. She gives him the encouragement, the emotional support to venture out onto the blanket, to reach for an unknown object, to try standing up. For the children this is a template for operating in the world in a respectful, reciprocal way. As the baby's visit unfolds, the children talk about what the baby is doing and feeling. The instructor and the baby's parent enrich the discussion by giving them the language of feeling—not to define what the children are feeling but to open up for them the vocabulary of emotions. The social evidence is there before them, all the material for understanding the rhythm of the parent–baby relationship.

Our program's approach speaks to the affective, or caring, side of children's development. It is designed to give children a living example of this child–parent relationship and what it means to be a parent. The baby is the teacher here; the baby's activities, responses, emotions and stages of development are the starting point, the base from which we build emotional literacy, learning the language of feeling from the baby's every move. Each month for the whole school year the baby's visit to the classroom inspires the kind of excitement, wonder and quest for understanding that we wish would always fill our children's school days. Teachers tell me that Roots of Empathy days are times when the children in the classroom are at their united, happy best.

The story I hear from every one of our classrooms is full of the magic the baby inevitably creates around him. Despite the fact I am a mother and an educator who has worked with babies and young children throughout my career, I am constantly amazed at the power of the baby. So often the baby seems to instantly recognize which child needs a smile or some special attention. Carla, who had poor verbal skills and many problems in the classroom, was sitting as patiently as she could at the edge of the blanket when the baby decided to crawl for the very first time—the baby crawled right to Carla. Her face lit up with joy. For months afterwards, when the Roots of Empathy instructor came to the class, she'd say to her, "Remember when Baby Cooper crawled right to me?"

Fraser never spoke in class. While he seemed to enjoy Amanda's visits, hovering close to the baby at every opportunity, he still didn't utter a word. Finally, at the fourth visit, while Amanda was being zippered up in her yellow snowsuit, she smiled directly at Fraser. He reached out, patted her on her tummy and said, "Nice baby." It was halfway through the school year and these were the first words his teacher and classmates had ever heard him speak. The pure human connection offered by the baby broke through Fraser's isolation.

Every child gets a chance to evaluate the program. While older children can write their thoughts, kindergarten children are asked to draw their favourite moment. Many of them choose the moment when they meet the baby in the circle. Another popular choice is one of the baby's milestones—"When the baby sat up," "When the baby smiled at me," "When the baby threw a ball to me." Still other children, fascinated by the interaction between baby and parent, will draw "When Mommy hugs the baby."

Creating the Future

I see this program as a practical strategy that has the power to break patterns of violence and poor parenting that have been passed down from generation to generation. A school year is a very long time in the life of a child. Giving that child the opportunity to be involved for a whole year with a parent and baby who model a healthy, nurturing relationship is an experience that sinks deeper than words or theories ever will. In the Roots of Empathy classroom, when we talk to the children about the importance of not shaking a baby, for example, they link that information on an emotional level to the baby they have come to know and care about. This isn't an imaginary baby who might be harmed by being shaken, this could be their class's real baby. The lesson sticks and the children apply it well beyond the classroom. I've even been told of six-year-olds in our Roots of Empathy class who have given "safe baby" tips to pregnant women in supermarket line-ups. The learning transforms from the inside out.

In the final Roots of Empathy session of the year, the children will write down on paper leaves their wishes for the baby they have come to know and care about. The leaves will hang on a Roots of Empathy wishing tree. The wishes are rich in compassion, optimism and hope. They are full of insight but also full of reflection. Children will frequently wish that the baby never has to endure the things that trouble their own childhood; for some that is bullying, for others it's standardized testing. Older children tend to express wishes that relate to the healthy environment or peaceful world they want for the baby. The wishes become a heartfelt legacy for the parents, but the thought that goes into making the wishes also helps the children to recognize that infants become children and eventually adults. Each baby is, quite literally, the future. What we do with our babies and children today determines the future of our community, our country and the world.

Leaves from the Wishing Tree

"My wish for Jordan is that he can be nice to people and help them. I wish that he can help people when they are sick to get better." (*Kindergarten*)

"Tristan, I wish that your family is still altogether and that you don't lose your daddy. My daddy died." (*Grade 1*)

"My wish for Silas is Peace, Food, Life, Toys, Freedom, House, Rest, Good Clothes, Water that is clean, Clean Air." (*Grade 2*)

"I wish that Jade will be loved and stay safe." (*Grade 3*)

"I wish for Ella not to fail her EQAO testing." (*Grade 3*)

"Courtney, here's my wish for you: Forgive your own mistakes." (*Grade 4*)

"Cole, I wish that you will know how to deal with bullies." (*Grade 5*)

"I wish that Madelyn would smile forever and never stop smiling. Her smile would cheer up the world." (*Grade 6*)

"I wish for Sashca to never give up on anything." (*Grade 7*)

"I wish Eli love. I wish Eli a wonderful life full of new experiences, good times, and an understanding of people's feelings. May you make many friends and few foes. Just remember to treat people the way you would like to be treated." (*Grade 8*)

SECTION TWO

The Six Strands
of Connection

4

ROOTS OF EMPATHY: SIX STRANDS OF HUMAN CONNECTION

T HROUGH OBSERVATION of the physical, cognitive, social and emotional growth of an infant during her first year of life, Roots of Empathy weaves together the strands of human connection that are critical for understanding ourselves, one another and the society we live in. But in the Roots of Empathy program understanding is only the first step. We work with children to take this understanding, open it out and build on it to imagine and create a better future.

In the following six chapters we will explore what each strand contributes to the development of empathy and human connection.

Strand 1: Neuroscience

The brain is a majestic organ. At no time is it more ripe for tuning than in the first years of life. The pathways that determine our ability to learn, to regulate our emotions, to respond to stress are formed at this stage with profound implications for our long-term success, the quality of our relationships and our health. Teaching children how the brain develops may seem an ambitious project for a Grade 1 class, but that is precisely what happens in the Roots of Empathy classroom. Children readily grasp the intimate connection between the parent's empathic, nurturing response to an infant and the excitement of exploration experienced by the infant. They see it happening before their eyes.

Strand 2: Temperament

Key to the development of empathy is the ability to understand a situation from another person's point of view, and that ability goes hand in hand with a sense of how our innate temperament determines our responses to particular situations. One of the approaches to learning more about the baby in the Roots of Empathy classroom is to explore the baby's temperamental traits. Each of us enters the world with a unique temperament and this influences, among other things, our level of activity, how we cope with change and how easily we are frustrated. Children move from observation of the baby's temperament to discussion of their own temperament. This builds understanding in the classroom and, more importantly, hones empathic skills as the child works out that, depending on temperament, he and his classmates will approach situations differently and have different emotional reactions.

Strand 3: Attachment

In our program, children are coached to observe the baby's attachment or development of trust in relation to his parent. By this I mean that the baby learns to trust that his parent will respond in predictable ways to the baby's needs. Our emotional development as human beings is fundamentally influenced by the strength of this relationship. It is how we learn to control and regulate our emotions. In the classroom, as children witness the empathic link between parent and infant, they are increasing their understanding of the complex world of emotions and, at the same time, assimilating a concept of competent parenting.

Strand 4: Emotional Literacy

Knowing how to read and write is one kind of literacy, usually the kind our school system is principally concerned with. Also important—I would argue more so—is literacy of feelings. We put a wide world of control and confidence in the hands and hearts of our children when we teach them how to identify and name emotions and how to use language or art or storytelling to convey their feelings. In the Roots of Empathy classroom, children observe how the baby expresses emotions and what those emotions are. This learning is extended as they are encouraged to reflect on their own emotions and discuss awareness of other people's emotions. The vocabulary of feelings is employed to show children a way to express their emotional experience and to convey how they feel about issues and events in the world around them. Through the sharing that occurs, children learn how the ability to verbally communicate emotion builds healthy relationships and a stronger, more confident sense of self.

Strand 5: Authentic Communication

We live in an era of unprecedented modes of communication. Satellite hookups can show us a reporter describing the devastation of the bombing of Kabul while it is happening behind him, a teleconference allows business associates to meet electronically across several time zones. And yet, paradoxically, we live in an era when we have never felt so alone: traditional family and community networks have become an endangered species, and we feel isolated from human understanding, where we are "lost in translation." Yet what makes us human is our ability to use language to convey fine nuances of thought and feeling, to achieve a meeting of minds and hearts. In our program, we honour the principle of authentic communication. This means that, as adults, we do not ask questions to which we already know the answers. It does mean that our questions provoke reflection and encourage a child's critical thinking and imagination. It means that the adult does not hide behind the formal persona of the grown-up or the expert, but honestly reveals his feelings when the context requires it and when to do otherwise is disrespectful to the child. Admitting to a child that there are times when we have been afraid, far from unsettling the child, inspires confidence that everyone can be afraid and that everyone can overcome it. When this happens, the learning experience is enriched and the validity of the child's emotional response is strengthened.

Strand 6: Social Inclusion

Every human being has a deep need to be heard, to be seen, to belong. A fundamental value in Roots of Empathy is inclusion. We create an environment where everyone has a voice, where every contribution has meaning. We work with children to break down barriers, encourage communication and acceptance, and create in the classroom a microcosm of democracy and collaboration. The lessons—on respect for individual temperament, responsiveness to the feelings of others, seeing the world from another person's perspective—come together to build a community within the classroom.

It may seem like a cliché to point out that so much of the strife in our communities and in our world today can be linked to an intolerance for any person or group or religion or nation that is different from ourselves. The sad fact remains that we are still light years away from bringing long-lasting solutions to what we can all recognize as a problem. A focus on empathy is a focus on our common experiences, on what unites rather than divides us. This commonality connects us, and not only vastly outweighs the differences but allows us to see differences in a new light. When we recognize this, we can see the differences for what they really are—a layering of richness into our lives, that gives us new ways of examining our relationships and our world.

5

LOVE GROWS BRAINS: TEACHING CHILDREN NEUROSCIENCE

IN THE FIRST SESSION between the students and the Roots of Empathy instructor—before they actually meet the baby—the instructor asks the children what they think the baby will be able to do. The younger children may say anything from walking and talking to eating spaghetti. In one junior kindergarten class, a little girl said, "The baby can smell the mommy."

This little girl's comment makes us smile. It is also loaded with insight. New babies experience the world in basic, physical ways—touch, taste, sound, sight, smell—but those experiences are the foundation of all the rapid and intricate brain development that will occur over this baby's early years.

A six-week-old puppy is not just a roly-poly bundle of playfulness, he is also a remarkably self-sufficient creature. He can walk, run, and even climb stairs if he encounters any; he has all the basic skills he needs to hunt or scavenge for food. In contrast, a six-week-old baby is completely helpless. She is totally dependent on others to bring her food, to keep her safe, even to move her to another position if she's uncomfortable. Although her brain has been growing since she was a minuscule embryo, at birth her brain functions include essential survival reflexes such as rooting, grasping, crying, sleeping, sucking—primarily functions of the brain stem and spinal cord—and an ability to express basic emotions such as joy, fear, affection, disgust and anger—due to the early stage of development of her limbic system. Even at six weeks the cerebral cortex, the part of her brain responsible for thinking, feeling and memory, is still in a very early stage of development. The knowledge we now have about brain development has changed the old "nature versus nurture" debate into a discussion about which genetic endowments will be expressed as a result of the child's early experiences.

The hundred billion neurons a baby was born with will, over the next several years, undergo an exuberant process of synaptic connection to build and strengthen the neurons into a complex network of nerve pathways. Her cerebral cortex will triple in thickness in her first year of life, and by the time she is eighteen months old her brain will weigh almost two-thirds of its eventual adult weight.[1] The brain is an experience-dependent organ, and during this amazing period of growth the baby's brain is more receptive to learning through nurturing, enriching experiences than at any other time in her development. Conversely, it is also a time of great vulnerability, when a lack of nurturing and lack of stimulation can compromise her potential.

Love Grows Brains

The newborn's brain is filled with sensory, motor, emotional and cognitive pathways poised to be shaped and modified based on every experience she has during the first few years of life. These experiences, from splashing in water to hearing a song or manipulating a toy, will repeatedly stimulate and solidify some synapses or neural connections but not others. Those that are rarely or never stimulated will eventually be "pruned" away. This is a good thing since it means that the efficiency of the stimulated connections is increased and strengthened. For example, research indicates that all babies are born with the potential to identify all the sounds in all human languages. [2] In the baby born to an English family, the pathways recognizing sounds used only in the !Kung language will gradually disappear, since those sounds are never heard, or are heard once in a while but have no particular meaning to the baby. Others will become super-highways, because the experiences they represent are repeated so often and are so important to the baby. The sounds of the baby's name, for example, will be recognized and deeply imprinted into the brain, so that she will later recognize her name instantly, even when it's called across a crowded, noisy room. The children in the Roots of Empathy class see many examples of the strength of what the baby has learned over the year they have spent together. By the end of the year, the greeting song, "Hello, Baby, How Are You?" which they sing to the baby at each visit, has become so recognizable that the baby perks up and smiles with joyful anticipation, as if it is her very own national anthem.

The initial helplessness and immaturity of human babies leads to a long-term benefit: the longer brain-development period experienced by humans means they can learn and adapt to a greater extent than any other animal. Most animals have brains that are already hard-wired to perform the functions they need: identify and hunt food, seek out an appropriate place to live, find a mate, avoid predators. The human infant needs to learn all those things, but is able to learn them in context, so that one baby figures out how to survive in conditions of arctic cold and another adjusts to tropical heat. The exceptional plasticity of the brain in the early years allows this to happen. Even more importantly, the brain continues to be adaptable, so that the adult whose environment changes dramatically at different points in his life can learn quickly how to adapt to the new environment.

The past few decades have witnessed enormous gains in what we know about how the brain functions. New positron emission tomography (PET) scans now allow us to see images of a living, active brain, and have taught us about the exponential growth of the infant brain in the years following birth. There is a crucial relationship between the child's experience, as mediated by a loving, nurturing adult in that child's life, and all the many aspects of human development—be they cognitive, sensory, emotional or physical. When we understand how important the early years are in the ultimate development of the child and the adult he will become, we will see that this is a lot more than just an interesting addition to our scientific knowledge. It is about economics, health, education, policy-making and the future of our society. What happens to our babies and small children has a lasting effect for generations and affects everyone's future. In Roots of Empathy we are very conscious that the children in the desks are the parents and decision-makers of tomorrow.

While few parents see themselves as neuroscientists, most have an awareness of the crucial impact experience has on the development of their children in the early years. It is important, however, not to see this unprecedented period of brain growth as a good time in the child's life to stuff him full of facts. You can buy flash cards and computer programs to teach the baby letters of the alphabet or the numbers from one to ten. But the brain develops as a network of interconnected pathways, and teaching babies these isolated facts, these separate chunks of disparate information, devoid of context, only creates little no-exit cul-de-sacs. Learning needs connection, and it is only through a variety of real-life experiences that babies are able to establish a well-connected network in their brains, ready to receive all the new information that will come their way as they grow. Those learning experiences, though, must happen in the context of a relationship; babies learn deeply through the modelling provided by parents. It is one of the truly remarkable aspects of human nature that babies are hard-wired to love those who take care of them, just as we, as parents, have a strong instinct to respond to the baby's needs, to comfort and talk to him, to play with him and to protect him.

Emotion is deeply intertwined with every piece of information the baby gathers. A baby learns and adapts the cultural attitudes and values of his family by osmosis, not in words but in the scent of daily interaction. He may be non-verbal but he can read emotions perfectly. In our program, as we talk about the important role of parents, we tell the children that a parent controls what happens in the baby's world and that the baby is dependent on the parent for everything. Before the baby comes in to visit, we tell them that the most significant thing they will see that day is the relationship between the mother and baby. It is this relationship, in which the baby gives the mother cues about what he needs and the mother responds to those cues, that sets the stage for everything the baby learns about his world. We tell the children that when they see the father hug the baby, the baby's brain is growing. When the mother sings to the baby, the baby's brain is growing. The brain responds to inputs from the senses and forms synaptic connections—"the neurons that fire together wire together." Feeling safe, secure and loved awakens all the baby's senses, and he is ready to drink in information. This relationship between parent and baby creates the environment that stimulates brain development and maximizes the child's potential for learning. One principal told me: "Roots of Empathy is the only program I know that teaches neuroscience to kindergarten students." He added a wish that his teachers understood as much about human development as his Roots of Empathy students did.

In the Absence of Positive Nurturing

We emphasize with students how important it is to be gentle with babies and small children. When young children are hit or abused repeatedly, the structure of their brain becomes increasingly diminished. They become intensely focused on the single task of avoiding pain. Often they become super-sensitive and vigilant to the environmental cues that signal danger to them: a change in the tone of a parent's voice, the sound of heavy steps on the stairs to the bedroom. If the abuse is unpredictable, as it usually is, the child's hyper-vigilance becomes heightened still more, in an attempt to find patterns and thus protection. This acute sensitivity comes at a great cost—the loss of the important pathways that might have connected to many other areas of learning. I could liken it to the effect of watching television. Whether or not the TV shows are harmful, there is no doubt that watching them robs the child of time that could otherwise be spent in positive social interaction or physical activities or games with real imaginative scope. This is non-recoverable time stolen from the child's opportunities to develop as a full human being.

A study by Seth Pollak at the University of Wisconsin found that most preschoolers can easily recognize whether photos of adult faces are showing happy, sad, angry or other feelings.[3] Preschoolers who had been abused, however, were likely to see even neutral or calm expressions as threatening. Seth Pollak observed, "It may be the case that physically abused children develop a broader category of anger because it is adaptive for them to notice when adults are angry." Imagine what that means to a child, and later an adult. Long after the actual abuse has ended, they go through life misinterpreting the emotions of others, seeing threats and danger where none exist, and often striking out to protect themselves. That is why, in Roots of Empathy classes, much effort goes into discussing *intention*.

It is important to be able to read the intentions of others. Students who have behavioural problems are frequently impulsive and less likely to reflect on what the mental state of another person might be. The ability to attribute mental states to others as a way of understanding their social behaviour is learned from infancy and enhanced by positive experiences in the environment in which we grow up. This ability is key in successfully discerning what another person intends by what he says or does. Without it, an aggressive child is more likely to believe that an accidental collision in the school hallway is an act of aggression and respond in kind. This can translate into "You bumped into me, so I'll shove you back." When this kind of scenario is discussed in our classrooms, children have an opportunity to reflect on the possible intentions of the person who did the bumping. This exploration opens new possibilities for understanding and can lead to a conclusion that the hallway collision was, indeed, an accident and that the child involved is sorry or embarrassed.

Many women who abuse their children lack empathy—the capacity to understand and respond to the feelings of others—and lack the ability to accurately identify the emotions revealed in facial expressions. They may, for example, confuse fear with anger. That's one reason why we teach our students about reading the cues of the baby. It is why a lot of time is devoted to discussing the baby's facial expressions and understanding what the baby is trying to tell us. We often ask the students, "If the baby could talk, what do you think she would say to us?" In the class that takes place the week after this family visit, the exploration of reading facial expressions is taken a step further. In small work groups, the students discuss illustrations we have created of children their own age exhibiting a variety of facial expressions and body stances. Although the children in the sketches have different physical features, hairstyles and clothing, pairs of the children will resemble each other in terms of the emotion they are exhibiting. The task for the students is to name each emotion and come to an agreement on which two children are exhibiting the same emotion. The discussion that flows from this activity engages the students in a rich exchange and exploration of nuances of feeling, for example, how anger differs from fear or sadness.

Chronic stress also compromises the developing structure of an infant's brain. When babies experience stress, the adrenal gland releases a surge of the stress hormone cortisol. Studies show that these high levels of cortisol have a negative effect on brain growth, slowing down the effectiveness of the electrical activity connecting neurons.[4] High levels of secretion of cortisol are also associated with depression. A baby doesn't have to be physically hurt or abused to experience stress. Because babies are aware of their helplessness and dependence on others, simply being separated from parents or familiar nurturing caregivers can be a significant source of stress. Even in cases where life circumstances prevent a mother from developing an attachment to her baby, the baby will still develop an emotional attunement to his mother and this mismatch between the baby's needs and the mother's response presents an increased risk for chronic stress.

Babies need responsive care. If a baby cries, for example, and no one responds, this is stressful for the baby, who relies on adults to provide comfort, food, stimulation and protection from the world. Crying is her first language, her most effective way of having her needs met, and if this is ignored she will feel abandoned and helpless. We now know that when babies are repeatedly stressed, either through unresponsive care or because of abuse, pathways in their brains begin to affect the biological pathways that have an impact on physical and mental health. When they grow up, these babies are at risk for a range of chronic health problems, including coronary heart disease, depression, memory loss, obesity and type II diabetes.

In one theme of the Roots of Empathy program we focus on crying and the importance of responding when a baby cries. We teach the children that babies cry because they have a problem. At this stage, lessons encourage children to reflect on why a baby might cry. What the children have been learning about the development of a baby's brain and about crying as a language to express needs leads them to attach meaning to the "noise," and to respect the baby's efforts to be understood. Respect for the baby engenders respect for one another.

Even in kindergarten, children can come up with a list of reasons why a baby might cry that is stunning in its insights. Equally stunning is the list of suggestions about how to respond when a baby cries: sing to the baby, change his diaper, she needs her mommy so give her back to her mommy. One instructor, during a session without the mother and baby, was holding one of the special Roots of Empathy dolls as she pretended to be a mother whose baby had been crying for a long time. In the role-playing, she told the class of Grade 5 students that she was feeling exhausted and needed a break. She asked one of the boys to look after the baby for her, then got up to organize a video for the class. When she looked back, the boy had moved the doll from a cradle hold to the football hold she had taught him and was gently patting the doll's back. He looked up at her with a big smile. As the video started, the boys in the class carefully passed the doll to one another, trying the different ways they had been shown to hold and comfort the doll. The self-consciousness you might expect was nowhere in sight—they were focused on solving the problem of the crying baby. One child described what he was doing as practicing to be an uncle. Another child said he was going to be a father of four when he grew up.

A Stimulating Learning Environment

As we coach children to observe the opportunities for learning that permeate the ordinary world of the baby, we are conveying that day-to-day living is the baby's laboratory. What do you imagine a learning environment looks like for a young child? A room with the latest computer equipment and educational software, math workbooks, microscopes and dissecting tools? How about a bedroom with a big cozy bed, a pile of picture books and a parent or grandparent to read stories? Or how about a kitchen floor with a parade of ants heading to the back door? Yes, that's a wonderful learning environment for a toddler. I have an infestation of ants in my kitchen right now, in fact. And a toddler, seeing those ants, would be fascinated. He'd get down on the floor and watch where they were going and see what they were carrying, and put small obstacles down in front of them to see if they'd climb over. You can keep a toddler amused for half an hour or longer with a good ant infestation.

What makes that a good learning environment is the response of the adults, because adults mediate children's learning experience. One mother will see the toddler gazing at the ants and say, "Yuck, dirty ants!" and squash as many as she can underfoot. Another will say, "Ants! Now that's interesting? What do you think they are doing? Where are those ants going?" and watch with her child. Maybe they'll even go to the library the next day and find a book or video about ants. Not only is the child learning a lot about some very intriguing insects, he knows that his interest in them will be respected and encouraged. When you capitalize on a child's interests, the child learns that life is interesting. That sets the stage for still more learning. A young child feels competent when he has successful interactions with people and is encouraged to explore. Curiosity and imagination are key features of optimal development in the early years. Nurturing the spontaneous interests of a child, as well as reinforcing strong neural connections, teaches them that they are interesting people and that "finding out stuff" is fun.

You can also contrast the cumulative language experience of the children in the two situations. There are many more words involved in the positive discussion of life as an ant than in the "Yuck, dirty ants" response. Children also learn that they can engage the adults in their lives in a positive way through talk. There's a lot going on in this ordinary, everyday chat about ants. The child is developing self-esteem and learning to solve problems—learning how to learn.

In my work with parenting programs where I developed family literacy initiatives, I have always encouraged parents not only to read to their children but to show their children how much they, as adults, enjoy reading. While flash cards and Bach immersion leave no lasting impression, the brains of very young children are stimulated by language. Of all the things a parent can do to foster cognitive development in these years of rapid brain growth, this, and reading are the most important. Children who have been engaged by their parents in reading and talking and singing demonstrate higher linguistic skills than children who have not had this kind of stimulation. Even twenty minutes a day reading with your child will make a noticeable difference to his vocabulary and school readiness, and just as importantly, the total sensory experience will influence his overall approach to learning. When parents sing with their baby and do finger plays and action songs, where the actions are reinforcing the meaning of the words in the songs, the baby's brain is active and growing.

When your preschooler stacks blocks into a tower, she is learning how one block added to another creates a tower of two blocks. That's addition. A little later she might try to make another tower the same height, so she can place a rectangular block on top and make a bridge. Now she has to make sure both towers are the same height. Is her tower of two blocks as tall as her tower of three blocks? No, it isn't, and when she puts the rectangle on top it falls off. She's learning about more and less, equations and inequations. What does she have to do to make the towers match? Add one block to the shorter tower? Subtract one from the taller tower? Addition and subtraction. She learns all these things through trial and error and experience, and when she begins to explore abstract math in school, she already has a strong foundation of experience to base her future learning on.

What I have described is play-based problem-solving. When children can tackle the problems in the playroom, the problems in the boardroom are manageable. Through these early experiences, the child develops a sense of competence. Preschoolers' play is too often passed off as unimportant. I've heard parents say they didn't like a certain preschool because "the children are just playing and it's a waste of their time." Nothing could be further from the truth. Play is the work of childhood. It is the best possible use of a young child's time and it is the gateway to learning; play-based problem-solving is the process by which children discover their world and their abilities.

Understanding Neuroscience: A Political Act

As I have illustrated, many of the everyday play activities young children enjoy are also teaching them about science and math. Mustard and McCain in their *Early Years Study* explain that play is the basis for learning in these early years, because it is how children experience, discover and explore the world around them.[5] This study could be described as an exhortation to governments to get on board with the connection between effective parenting and infant brain development, an exhortation to invest in the first three years of life.

Learning how to learn is caught, not taught. It is a value, or an approach to life, which is intrinsically learned through many repeated experiences that reinforce the value of curiosity and imagination. In my parenting programs, I used to "workshop" activities to encourage parents to become childlike and follow the lead of the child, supporting the child's natural interest with just the right measure of added information or probing questions and comments. Parents are the models from whom children learn if life is exciting or tiresome. If a parent lives life through a TV screen rather than fully, interactively engaging with life, this has a damaging effect on how the child perceives herself as a learner.

The ability of a parent to provide the stimulation a child needs to develop an enthusiasm for learning is not in itself a socioeconomic issue. It can, however, become a political issue when chronic poverty casts a pall over one's life, eroding the joy associated with having a young child, when a lack of basic necessities reduces the day to a round of exhaustion, frustration and depression, regardless of the parent's education or prior life experiences. In this context, early brain development is very much a political issue with huge economic, cultural and moral implications. As a child growing up in Newfoundland, I frequently heard the expression "there is no point in crying for cabbage if you planted corn." Apply this to human potential and it is clear that we cannot reap what we failed to sow.

As every neuroscientist and knowing parent will affirm, the early years really do cast a long shadow—one that stretches across the child's lifetime. The old question of nature versus nurture is no longer a matter of serious debate. We now know that in the realm of brain development, the potential for nurture to profoundly enhance what nature gives us is enormous, exciting and an awesome responsibility. How that child is nurtured during the baby, toddler and preschool years will largely determine the shape and influence of that shadow. Building a stronger, safer, more caring world depends on what happens in the nursery.

It may seem like an ambitious undertaking to introduce elementary-school children to neuroscience, but Roots of Empathy's approach to parenting is grounded in an understanding of human development that recognizes the critical links between cognitive and emotional growth as the brain develops. The benefits for the children in the classroom are multilayered, immediate and far-reaching. In observing how the baby learns, the children gain insights about themselves and their own individual learning styles. They are also discovering a wonder and respect for the complex wiring that develops in the brain as a result of apparently simple everyday experiences—the concept that love grows brains. In learning about the symbiotic relationship between the parent and baby and its impact on optimal brain growth, they are learning about the vulnerability of babies and small children; at the same time, they are learning how critical it is to be a sensitive, vigilant and responsive parent when one takes on the responsibility of having a baby.

6

TEMPERAMENT: GETTING TO KNOW YOU

This baby cries because she is hungry.

*D*uring a Roots of Empathy session with a Grade 2 class, one little boy was fooling around, chatting animatedly to his friend and paying no attention to the opening moments of the lesson. The classroom teacher scolded him for his behaviour and told him he was not being polite to the Roots of Empathy instructor.

Brandon grinned at the instructor and said, "Oh, she understands. It's just my temperament." He knew the rules about settling down for the start of class, but what he had learned about his own temperament gave him confidence that the instructor would understand he was impulsive and that he wasn't trying to be rude and would have empathy for him.

What Is Temperament?

Nature gives us the predisposition to love, nurture and teach our babies, but the first months and years are a learning process as much for the parent as for the baby. If we are to feel competent in our parenting, there are important features of these small human beings that are important for us to know. As Brandon's story tells us, understanding temperament is a valuable insight and essential in building strong relationships.

In Roots of Empathy we teach children that babies are all born with different temperaments, and that the baby you get is rarely the baby you ordered. Any parent with more than one child can tell you that these differences in temperament are innate. Your first child, a boy, is born in the spring. You name him David. You take a year off work. You breastfeed him, play with him, read to him, sing to him, take him to the park. David feeds contentedly, sits happily on your lap, sits equally happily on the lap of your friends when they come to visit, goes to sleep easily and wakes up smiling. Three years later your second child, also a boy, is born in the spring. You name him Max. You take a year off work. You breastfeed him, play with him, read to him, sing to him, take him to the park. There the resemblance ends. Max fusses at your breast, turning his head at every sound; on your lap he wriggles and arches his back; he howls when you try to hand him over to your friend, screams when you put him in his crib, and starts crying as soon as he wakes up.

How on earth did this happen? You didn't move house—David and Max were born into an almost identical environment, except of course that David was born into a family of two and Max into a family of three. You were thrilled at their arrival in the world and were ready to provide the same loving parenting approach. The answer is both easy and difficult. David was born with a set of temperament traits that, among other things, predisposed him to adapt easily, to react well to change and to quietly enjoy his environment. Max arrived with a set of temperament traits that, among other things, made him more distractible, less welcoming of change and slower to develop regular patterns. What makes this an easy answer is that there is a solid genetic reason for the differences in your two boys—they were born that way, with a distinct set of temperament traits that exist regardless of the environment. What makes it a difficult answer is that the parenting approach that worked so well with David will need to be adjusted to accommodate Max's temperament.

When we discuss this concept with the children in the Roots of Empathy class, we are introducing them to the idea that, just as there are all kinds of different babies, there are also all kinds of different children and all kinds of ways to be a good parent. We want them to know that a competent parent can adjust to dealing with a baby who is very sensitive, or who is very irregular in her sleeping or eating patterns, or who is unusually active and energetic.

Parents who have babies with more "difficult" temperaments often worry that they are doing something wrong. They see other parents whose babies seem easy to care for, and they feel like failures. In fact, well-meaning family members or friends may even give them the impression that their baby's fussiness or irregularity is their fault. They may be told that their nervousness as new parents is transmitting itself to the baby and preventing the baby from settling into regular habits. Learning about the reality of temperament helps parents feel more competent, knowing that they are not bad parents, they simply have a baby who is different from them or different from the way they thought she would be. In my work with thousands of parents over the years, the single thing that brought them the most confidence was this explanation of temperament; it helped parents to recognize and discuss their baby's unique temperament and to realize that the way a baby faces the world is much more an outcome of unfolding than an outcome of moulding. As parents develop more confidence in the job of parenting, they can competently take on the role of mediating their child's behaviour to help socialize him for the world that is. By helping a child understand himself and his social context, parents can make life easier for their child, giving him a way to manage his innate disposition and interact with others more smoothly. If, for example, a child is high in intensity, she is more inclined to speak out immediately and loudly, often interrupting others; without help, she will have trouble socially. As parents we have to take steps to mediate, to help our child notice what is going on around her and develop the skills and self-awareness to be successful in her social milieu.

I would never try to give parents a recipe for how to raise or care for their children. Every family represents a unique set of relationships—there is no "best" parenting approach for that family. What I have found is that parents sigh with relief as they develop an understanding about the complex world of temperament: it gives them a different window to look through as they observe the miracle that is their child, a different perspective on the child's behaviour. It is another tool for getting to know their baby and enjoying their relationship with him.

In Roots of Empathy the exploration of temperament in the classroom opens the door to self-knowledge for the students and provides a new way for the students to understand and respect each other. For the teacher in the classroom, it can provide additional insights into students' behaviour. While teacher training includes information about learning modalities (e.g., kinesthetic versus auditory or visual learners), this can be insufficient help in the classroom; for example, a child who is low in adaptability can be thrown off for hours by a requirement to change abruptly from one activity to another. With an understanding of temperament the teacher will know that that child will manage better if given more lead time to cope with a change-over. Temperament is not just a learning style, it is our gut reaction, our responsiveness to the world at a cellular level.

I was once sitting in a circle with a group of kindergarten children towards the end of the school year, and I asked them what they thought would be different about going into Grade 1 in September. They talked about having recess, staying at school the whole day, bringing their lunch, getting homework. "And you won't have Mrs. G. as your teacher in Grade 1. You'll be getting a new teacher," I reminded them. One little boy, Dawson, was visibly dismayed by my words. "Will it be difficult for you to have a new teacher?" I asked him. Dawson nodded emphatically and told me, "Yes, I just won't go to Grade 1." In the circle we had a discussion about getting ready for new things and how it was easy for some people, hard for others, and how it gets better if you have time to think about it. Dawson's level of dismay began to decrease. Even at five, a child can derive comfort and a sense of control from the knowledge that he and lots of children like him naturally have difficulty with change, and that it is something that gets better when you can talk about it.

Understanding the inborn, individual differences that we describe in talking about temperament is very much a matter of respect and inclusion. In the Roots of Empathy classroom we respect babies for who they are. We are careful not to describe temperament traits in a blaming way or in a negative way—they are not good or bad, they simply are. We talk about temperament traits as being on a continuum. Some people are high in distractibility, some people are low, some people are in between. We also discuss how a trait that can cause difficulties in some circumstances can be very desirable in other instances. For example, a highly active person can be exhausting sometimes, but at other times can provide the energy to get things done when the pressure is on. In the learning community of the classroom, every person, every temperament has a part to play, every contribution is important and our differences are to be honoured. And yet, even as we use the language of temperament to understand and respect the ways we are different, we recognize that we are all on a continuum, and that the common ground of our shared experiences transcends differences and knits us together.

Over the course of the school year, as the children develop a relationship with "their" baby, they are encouraged to observe how the baby's behaviour illustrates her temperament. The discussion of temperament is entered into with tremendous enthusiasm by the children. The context is exploratory and non-judgmental. They delight in identifying their own temperament traits and illustrate these traits by sharing stories of what they did as babies or toddlers. These discussions not only increase self-reflection and, consequently, self-knowledge, but also engender an understanding of their classmates in a very positive way. The communication and dynamics in the group are enhanced, and the children tap into a human perspective that will help them throughout their lives.

Temperament is, of course, just one piece of the puzzle of understanding who we are as human beings. We are also shaped by our abilities and interests, our cultural heritage, and our home and family life—the infusion of race, religion, language, values, socioeconomics and all the other factors that determine how the family sees itself and how the children see themselves. Even temperament, innate as it is, can be intensified or modified by the kind of interaction a child has with his parents or by the child's broader social environment. One of the traits that tends not to change over time is activity level. Children learn how to manage their need to be active according to the situation. Some children obviously are more successful in tailoring their behaviour appropriately.

Temperament: How We Behave

Understanding temperament is key to understanding the way our children react in any given set of circumstances. As parents, we need this perspective to help us deal more effectively with our children and give them strategies that will take them into a successful adulthood.

A low-activity child, for example, is more likely to choose sedentary pursuits like reading. This can be a blessing for a parent who is busy preparing dinner. But chances are that this same child is also slow to get moving when it's time to leave the house and everyone gets frustrated waiting for her to get her shoes on. A parent who is sensitive to this trait in her child will give her early warning about the impending departure, so that the child has enough time to get ready and avoids the stress of being "hurried up" by impatient family members. With this kind of support, the child will learn that she needs extra time and plan for it. Her temperament trait does not become a "flaw" for which she constantly feels blamed.

Temperament Traits

The work of the child psychiatrists Stella Chess and Alexander Thomas identifies nine distinct temperament traits.[1] The degree to which we have a particular temperament trait in our genetic make-up varies from person to person. One person may have a high level of "adaptability" and a low level of "distractibility," while another person has these same traits in an inverse level of intensity. This research on temperament is used in the Roots of Empathy program to help students understand the baby's behaviour and reactions and to illuminate their own uniqueness. The nine traits are commonly described as Activity Level, Intensity, Sensitivity, First Reaction, Adaptability, Mood, Frustration Reaction,

Distractibility and Rhythmicity. The training we provide to our instructors includes a module on how to use temperament theory to support the development of emotional literacy and empathy.

ACTIVITY LEVEL

The baby with a high activity level will be active, enthusiastic and squirmy when held; she will likely try to climb out of the high chair or splash everyone in the room at bath time. Once this baby masters rolling over, she'll often use it as a way to get to toys or just to explore the room, and she can hardly wait to start crawling! As she grows into childhood she will be eager to play active games and sports, and will find it difficult to sit still in the classroom for more than short periods of time. She is the child who wiggles around in her chair, taps her fingers or toes while the teacher is talking, and is first out the door when recess is announced.

The baby with a lower activity level will move more slowly and less often, being content to sit in a high chair or on a parent's lap. He can roll over, but doesn't do it very often—he's usually happy to stay in the position in which he was placed. When he grows older, this child will sit quietly for long periods of time looking at books or working on puzzles.

INTENSITY

Intensity refers to the strength of a person's response to situations—either positive or negative. The intense baby will cry loudly and energetically when upset, and squeal with joy when delighted. As he grows older, he tends to see situations in dramatic contrast: as either wonderful or disastrous. There is rarely a middle ground.

The less intense baby is mellow and more subtle in her response to situations. Her reactions tend to be mild—she will fuss a bit when hungry instead of crying vigorously, and smile rather than laugh when something pleases her. In a busy family, this may result in her getting less attention than more intense siblings, and, as a child, she may be mistakenly seen as unenthusiastic.

SENSITIVITY

The highly sensitive baby is keenly aware of her surroundings and feels and reacts strongly to sensory input such as noises, cold, heat, texture, soiled diapers, and how she is handled. These babies become children who can't stand the way the label on the inside of the T-shirt scratches, or the way the seams on their socks feel on their toes. They often ask to wear fleece sweatpants instead of jeans. They may be acutely sensitive to lighting or room temperature.

Babies with a less sensitive temperament can sleep through loud noises and are not bothered by wet or dirty diapers. As they grow, they don't notice what kind of sheets are on the bed or care if they wear jeans or fleece. Often they are not especially sensitive to cold and wonder why you want them to put on a sweater.

FIRST REACTIONS (APPROACH OR WITHDRAWAL)

Some babies respond positively to new people and new situations. They will smile and reach out to a stranger, quickly pick up a new toy and respond with delight when offered a new kind of food. As older children, they find it easy to speak to new classmates and to make friends. They are eager to try new activities and tend to be strongly attracted to the "new and different," occasionally with an impulsiveness that can lead them into danger.

The more cautious babies will resist new people and new situations. Offer them a taste of pear when they've never tried pear before, and they'll spit it out or push the spoon away. Introduce them to Grandma, who is visiting from England, and they'll turn away and bury their head in your shoulder. They are likely to be just as cautious about starting school or changing to a new teacher and classroom when graduating to the next grade. It takes these children longer to make friends, and they may resist visiting their friends' homes or going for sleepovers.

ADAPTABILITY

This refers to the ease with which a person adjusts to a situation. Very adaptable babies find transitions effortless and are not bothered by change. They can sleep as readily in a laundry basket at Grandma's as in their crib at home. This baby becomes the child who "goes with the flow" and easily fits into changing plans. Call him for dinner, and he has no problem leaving the game he was playing and joining the rest of the family at the table.

The less adaptable baby is unsettled by transitions. This is the baby who starts to cry immediately when she wakes up, and who needs lots of support and help to fall asleep. As she gets older, being called to dinner when she is watching TV can cause a meltdown. She will get upset when plans change, and be very disappointed when an anticipated event doesn't take place. Even making the transition back to school after a weekend at home can be difficult, and going back after the Christmas holidays, March break or summer vacation may create challenges.

MOOD

The baby's mood refers to his general disposition. The baby whose mood is predominantly positive is frequently described as "sunny"—the kind of baby who feels happy, smiles most of the time and is very friendly. The cheerful baby becomes a child who is outgoing and optimistic, makes friends easily, and expects things to turn out for the best.

The baby whose mood is generally more negative will cry readily, and her facial expressions tend to be serene or even serious. She becomes a child who seems reserved when meeting new people and who may complain about small things. She often appears to be daydreaming or lost in contemplative thought. Just because this child doesn't smile and laugh as readily as others, though, doesn't mean she's unhappy. She just has a more serious demeanour.

FRUSTRATION REACTION/PERSISTENCE

This is the trait that describes how we respond to situations that are not easily resolved and challenge our persistence. The baby who is very persistent will stick with a task—like learning to walk—even when there are obstacles such as slippery floors and little legs that aren't quite ready to keep him balanced. As a child, this persistent person will tackle learning activities with equal attention and focus. For example, he will be able to overcome the frustration of initial mistakes and learn to play a musical instrument successfully. This trait can lead to challenges too. A parent will have a difficult time keeping the persistent child away from things that grab her attention—including electrical outlets. The persistent child can also get very frustrated when the routines of school interfere with his desire to see something through to completion.

The easily frustrated baby will quickly become upset when she can't readily master a task. When she has difficulty manoeuvring the toy figure into the truck, she might simply give up, or she might cry or throw the figure away in anger. In later years, she will be more likely to drop out of a sport if she doesn't experience success right away and may not stay focused on a math problem until she solves it. This child requires consistent encouragement to maintain interest in challenging activities.

DISTRACTIBILITY

This is the degree to which we are able to be distracted by outside stimuli from what we are currently doing. A baby with high distractibility is easy to redirect. If she is crawling towards a shiny but breakable ornament, her mother can capture her attention by offering a toy instead. As the easily distracted baby grows older, homework and paying attention in school may be a challenge, as there are many things to notice that keep the child from maintaining focus. A more positive feature of high distractibility is a facility for noticing the reactions of others and being more aware of the feelings at play.

The less distractible baby is not so easily diverted from something he has decided to do. One Roots of Empathy mother described finding her baby about to unplug a lamp cord; she brought him a toy and moved him into another part of the room. He ignored the toy and crawled back to the lamp. She picked him up and carried him into another room and tried to involve him in singing "Itsy Bitsy Spider." He pushed her hands away and crawled determinedly back to the lamp, ready to pull out the plug. When she closed the door to that room, he sat right beside it and cried. These babies are also often harder to soothe when upset. They are not distracted from discomfort or an unpleasant incident by being bounced or sung to, as a more distractible baby might be. As older children, they can focus on the task at hand despite many distractions—successfully completing their homework while the TV blares and siblings race around the room. While this ability to concentrate has many benefits, it can also present itself as being oblivious to other people and can be irritating to those who are trying to get the child's attention.

RHYTHMICITY OR REGULARITY

This describes the degree to which a baby's biological rhythms are regular and predictable. The regular baby will seem to have an internal alarm clock: he wakes up at the same time, wants to eat on a regular schedule, and is easily toilet-trained because that function, too, follows a predictable pattern. This infant naturally grows into a child who creates and follows routines easily, who is well organized, and whose behaviour continues to be predictable.

The less regular baby will take a two-hour nap today and be wide awake after twenty minutes tomorrow. Her parents never know when she'll be hungry or sleepy. She might space feedings an hour apart today and three hours apart tomorrow, or nurse every forty-five minutes all morning and take a four-hour nap in the afternoon. As she grows older, she may be disorganized with her toys and her school work, and find it hard to arrive on time for appointments. While her environment may work to help her adjust successfully to routines, it will always be more of a struggle for her than for a person whose temperament is naturally regular.

Temperament — The Big Picture

One of the heartening aspects of these temperament traits is that many of the qualities we often see as "negative" in babies turn out to be quite positive in older children or adults. The baby who is hard to distract, for example, can be tough for parents to manage, but when he grows up he'll be the one who can get things done despite a noisy classroom or chaotic work environment. The baby who is slow to adapt and fusses at changes in his environment can develop into a strong-willed person who has the courage of her convictions and is not easily swayed by the persuasions of others. It often helps parents who are dealing with a challenging baby to think about how these character traits can play out when their child is older. As we talk about this in the Roots of Empathy class-room, we see in some children an almost palpable dawning of relief. They grasp intuitively that a way of behaving that some-times gets them in trouble can also turn out to be a positive aspect of who they are.

In a Grade 7 class, the instructor was describing the tempera-ment trait associated with activity level. She talked about how the high-activity child is likely to shine on a sports team and is happiest out on the street playing hockey; given choices, the low-activity child will prefer to read a book or draw and is more likely to find success in activities that require contemplation and quiet creativity. Nathan, who had not previously been vocal in the class, asked, "Does that mean I'm not lazy?" The instructor later said that Nathan looked as if a huge weight had been lifted off his shoulders.

While I have described nine types of temperament traits, they tend to group themselves into three recognizable patterns, corresponding to whether a baby is easy to take care of, difficult to take care of, or somewhere in between. The good news is that only about 10 per cent of babies are considered to be "difficult." These are the babies who are highly active, very intense, negative in mood, low in rhythmicity and negative in their first reactions. They have a lot of difficulty in adjusting to a regular eating or sleeping schedule, cry frequently, "make strange" with new people, are slow to accept new situations and are easily frustrated. "Easy" babies make up the largest single grouping (about 40 per cent), and are considered low in intensity, positive in mood, very regular and predictable, and positive in their first reactions to new situations. They will smile readily, sleep at regular times, welcome new foods, adjust quickly to school, and fit in easily in social groups. About 15 per cent of babies have been identified as "slow to warm up." They adapt slowly but are low in intensity. They are not as regular in their routines as "easy" babies, but do not fuss as strongly as "difficult" babies. Outside of these three groupings are the babies who show combinations of traits that do not tend to one extreme or the other. "Difficult" babies are at a greater risk of abuse because they make parents feel like failures.

But how difficult or easy a baby is depends a lot on our expectations. In a culture where we tend to schedule every detail of our lives, a baby who does not follow a predictable routine in his eating and sleeping strikes a discordant note. In cultures where the clock is not followed so faithfully, parents find it easier to adapt to an irregular baby's unpredictability. In cultures where babies are kept close to their mothers day and night, a baby who is slow to warm up to new situations or dislikes strangers is less likely to have to deal with these situations, so it doesn't seem as much of a problem.

A great deal of research on temperament has been done around the world. Findings from Asia, Africa, Europe and North America confirm that the nine distinct temperament traits and predominant patterns documented by Chess and Alexander are universal. [2] In a world where we seem to struggle alone all too often, it is encouraging to know how much we, as human beings, are alike, sharing so many common traits that transcend culture, race and class.

How the Parent Adjusts to the Baby

In the Roots of Empathy classes, we also talk with the children about "goodness of fit." Parents have temperament traits too, and these can often be quite different from the baby's temperament traits. A baby who has difficulty establishing routines and is low on the continuum of regularity, for example, may put a great deal of stress on a parent who is high in rhythmicity and most comfortable with a regular schedule and routine. The father who is low in activity will find his very active baby exhausting to take care of. Parents who are very persistent have difficulty understanding why their toddler gives up on new tasks so quickly; their attempts to bring him back to the puzzle he was struggling with can end with him dissolving into a tantrum.

During a discussion on the baby's temperament, a Roots of Empathy mother told the class, "When I was at work, I could count on a definite routine. Meetings were at a scheduled time and lasted two hours. I knew that my weekly reports were due on Thursdays so I made sure to set aside time on Wednesday afternoons to complete them. All of that suited me really well. Before my baby was born, I suppose I imagined that I'd organize my days as a mom the same way I did at work. Then Katie came along! She's almost seven months old and we don't have a schedule yet. Some nights she sleeps all the way through and other nights she's ready to play at three o'clock in the morning. Then in the afternoon, I plan to go shopping after her nap. I'm all ready to go and she's sleeping soundly. But we're getting used to each other. I'm certainly learning to go with the flow!" Revelations like this bring home to the students not only the impact of temperament traits but the love that can make conflicts melt away.

Mismatches of temperament can have negative implications when the parents believe that the baby's behaviour—his irregular eating patterns, for example, or his lack of persistence—represents faults in the baby that they need to correct or improve. Even when we are happy that our child is strong in a particular trait, we can still face challenges. We may be glad that our child is persistent, for example, as we watch her solve a problem, but are less delighted as we observe this same persistence in a social context when she is insisting on her own way. We want to decree in what ways she persists. When parents see these qualities as innate traits with which their child came into the world, they can shift their focus.

"Goodness of fit" is not some immutable connection between parent and baby. It has to be worked with and adjusted as the parent–child relationship develops. For example, parents can help their children to manage those traits that are likely to have negative consequences on the ease with which the child will adapt to social situations. The intense child will always have a tendency towards strong reactions, but with support she can learn to express these in acceptable ways. Intensity of response can be the trigger for action that makes much-needed changes in our world. Dr. Martin Luther King in his speeches responded with intensity to the racism and intolerance that many others simply accepted, and he used his strong emotions to lead others into a new era of civil rights. Gandhi epitomized persistence in his untiring pursuit of non-violent resistance to injustice.

In my work with parents, I encourage them to take an inventory of their own temperaments and compare them to their baby's traits. Sometimes they are surprised to recognize similarities they hadn't acknowledged before, and sometimes they discover that different temperaments have been causing conflicts between them. Sometimes parents need to acknowledge the baby they dreamed of before they can fully accept the baby they have. It's natural for parents to imagine their baby in the months before birth, and the images we create are often strongly influenced by those soap-opera babies who take endless naps and coo happily on mother's lap in between. When the real baby turns out to be one who rarely sleeps and who cries for many hours out of the day, parents sometimes feel as though they were somehow given the wrong baby or that they are at fault. This wasn't what they had in mind. Many question why they became parents in the first place and doubt their ability to parent. The baby does not allow the parent to fulfill the dream of the parent he or she wanted to be.

Temperament in the Classroom

During one of our classes, a baby who was crawling around the room grabbed one of the children's name tags. Another child quickly held out a toy to the baby, and was able to exchange the toy for the name tag. The instructor was impressed by the child's quick thinking in employing this strategy with a baby who was susceptible to distraction.

Learning about temperament allows children to celebrate the unique make-up of the Roots of Empathy baby. We don't blame or criticize the baby for having a negative mood or a low frustration reaction. We enjoy her for who she is. This approach gives the children permission to be comfortable in their own skin, to understand their own reactions and to be respectful of the temperaments of others. An important aspect of empathy is the ability to understand why another person behaves as she does, an understanding that is enhanced by the discussion of temperament.

In learning about temperament, the children's learning follows these natural steps:

- understanding the temperament of the baby
- understanding their own temperaments
- understanding the temperaments of others

This is a pathway that parallels the development of empathy:

- observing and identifying the baby's feelings
- identifying and naming one's own feelings
- using this knowledge about feelings to be able to take the perspective of others and understand how they are feeling

The discussions about temperament give children a valuable vocabulary to express themselves and to express an understanding of others. Children begin to see all the shades of who they are and who they can be. This is further reinforced through the use of children's literature. Every experience that is arts-based builds a common mood, blending education of the mind and education of the heart, pushing cognitive growth. Through storytelling, the children are brought together in sharing common emotions, and touch on their own personal experiences as they talk about the story's theme. For example, in our theme about Sleep, we read *Franklin Has a Sleepover*, the story of the little turtle's first night away from home; the empathy the children feel for Franklin's experience is palpable.[3] They connect strongly to this story that touches on the trait of adaptability; they absolutely "get" his fears and apprehensions about new and strange situations and separation from the familiar. This story, like all literature, opens the door to feelings. It gives the children words to express their own emotions and to connect compassionately to one another in a shared emotional experience. The vulnerability of the little turtle strikes a chord that encourages even very shy children to express their feelings. In one class the *Franklin* story led to a child talking about bed-wetting. That level of disclosure underscores the sense of safety and trust among the children in the classroom. It bodes well for creating a society where sharing one's vulnerabilities is not a cause for shame, but a bridge of connection.

Teachers learn too. Teachers who have welcomed the Roots of Empathy program in their classrooms often find the lessons on temperament helpful in their accommodation of students' individual needs. Out of respect for their students' differences some teachers rethink how long they expect children to sit at their desks. Restlessness is not bad behaviour, it's not gender, it's genes. If the highly active child is not permitted to move about legitimately, she will move about anyway because she has to, and will get herself in trouble for rocking the chair or being where she should not be. The child who is low in persistence and easily frustrated will accomplish more if tasks can be broken down into smaller, easier-to-solve steps. He needs to experience success at each stage so that he can continue with the process. Doing it this way prepares him for managing more complex projects later in life.

Children with low regularity may not have felt hungry at breakfast, even though food was lovingly prepared for them. They may then be starving at nine-thirty; as their blood sugar drops they have little chance of learning and a much-increased chance of getting into an argument. This child needs food to be available for snacking. There is much to be gained from having snack foods such as carrots, apples, cheese and juice available in classrooms. When food is available in this way as a support to learning, it allows the child whose family can't provide adequate food and the child whose body doesn't acknowledge traditional eating schedules not to be penalized. This will make schools a more receptive place for real children who have different approaches to life and learning and different capacities for complying with the traditional expectations of formal schooling.

Temperament: Learning for Everyone

Temperament is addressed consistently throughout the Roots of Empathy program. It is not treated as an isolated body of information but is connected to a fuller understanding of how we come to be the unique and complex human beings we are. Exploring temperament allows the program to provide learning experiences for the parents, the teacher, the students and the baby. The baby, in his unique way, is learning all the time from everyone around him. Parents who have a baby with a number of difficult temperament traits learn the importance of accepting them and helping to manage them. Teachers who hear students reflect on their own temperaments can develop deeper understanding about their behaviour. As students acquire an array of knowledge about their own temperament, they can learn to expect certain reactions in themselves and find ways to mediate them. Instead of getting angry with a classmate who has a very low frustration level, they can figure out how to help her.

Identifying and understanding different temperaments honours individuality and invites consideration of others' perspectives. It gives children successful experience in seeing how differences and similarities work together to create room for everybody. The classroom, and the society it mirrors, is in a sense an orchestra: some musicians may be percussive and loud and some may be smooth and quiet, but the symphony is not complete without the contribution of every musician.

7

ATTACHMENT: BUILDING THE FIRST RELATIONSHIP

*O*ne of the Roots of Empathy instructors was holding the baby when he began to fuss. The mother told the instructor that Rafael liked to be held facing out, so she moved the baby into that position. Rafael continued to squirm and make unhappy noises. The instructor tried bouncing him gently up and down, but his unhappiness only increased. Finally some of the children said, "Give Rafael back to his mother." As soon as he was in his mother's arms again, the baby smiled.

The First Relationship — *The Foundation of a Healthy Society*

The illiterate of the next generation will not be those who don't know how to read, they will be those who don't know how to relate. Our ability to relate in a positive, healthy way with others goes back to the development of our very first relationship. In this scene from a Roots of Empathy classroom we have a baby giving us a "textbook" illustration of the strength of his first relationship in his secure attachment to his mother. A baby with a secure attachment often protests when separated from the person he loves and is quickly comforted and reassured once they are together again.

As we have seen in earlier chapters, babies are born with a number of basic capabilities and an array of distinct temperament traits. This genetic inheritance is mediated through our experience—the gifts of nature shaped by nurture in an intricate dance, creating pathways at a cellular level. How do we ensure that these crucial early experiences will lay a solid, positive foundation? We do it by supporting the highest and most influential point of impact—the attachment relationship. The quality of this relationship in the early years can dramatically affect how our genetic potential is realized.

The roots of empathy, the realization of human potential—all that we wish for in the world—are in this first relationship. A child's first attachment to a significant, reliable person is the basis for all the relationships of a lifetime. The success of this relationship has less to do with the family structure within which it develops—a two-parent family, a lone-parent family, same-sex parents—and everything to do with the quality of the relationship. Whatever its structure, the most valuable institution in nurturing attachment is the family. We work to preserve pure water through sound sanitation systems and meticulous monitoring of water quality. What about strong social environments? Do we go to the same lengths to implement supportive measures to shore up the health of our social environment and eradicate the toxins that undermine it? Do we work to maintain the social equity that ensures well-being and quality of life to be within everyone's reach? To do that, you have to have equity in the cradle and in the high chair; you have to create hope and opportunity for every child. You don't take the gun-registry approach, trying to get control after the fact. Real change comes from the front end, from prevention, from getting it right at the start, where it starts. This means supporting parenting capacity.

In my work with young parents who have grown up in an environment where violence is a mode of communication and where a consistent, nurturing style of parenting is a rare phenomenon, I have seen first-hand the damage inflicted when the sense of self-worth that is created in a secure early relationship is tragically missing. You'll remember Amy, the young mom I described in chapter 1. When I visited her, her face was badly bruised from recent punches; she opened the door to me, oblivious of the toddler clinging to her leg. She wanted to assure me that her partner didn't mean it, that he loved her. She was barely out of her teens and trapped in a belief that this was normal, that negative attention was inevitable, and better than no attention at all. Her acceptance of this belief had been passed on through the "see-saw" parenting she received from her own mother. She in turn was modelling this same behaviour for her toddler. Attachment gone wrong can unravel a person's life. That is why in the Roots of Empathy classroom, we consistently show how the attachment between the parent and the baby is the safety net in the baby's life.

What Is Attachment?

In the first year of life, infants depend on others for food, warmth and affection, and therefore must be able to trust completely that their parents (or other primary caregivers) will provide these. If their needs are met consistently and responsively by the parents, infants will not only develop a secure attachment with the parents, but will learn to trust their environment in general as well. Infants whose needs are met inconsistently, ignored or met only after long and unbearable delays may develop mistrust towards people and their environment, and even towards themselves.

The baby's first developmental imperative is to form an attachment, and the quality of this attachment is fundamental to the baby's learning and to all future relationships.

Attachment is frequently described as the enduring emotional bond between the child and parent, for which the stage is set from the moment the child is born and which grows in strength through the first year of life. It is a long-term process, a relationship created as the baby and parent communicate and respond to one another, a relationship built out of each interaction they have. In the first two years, as attachment grows, so does the baby's sense of security and confidence in being protected and comforted.

The earliest proponents of the importance of attachment[1] studied the behaviours of babies and parents in the crucial first year of the baby's life and drew significant conclusions about the way in which a baby attaches to her parent and how that process is influenced by the baby's experience of the parent's response to her needs.

When a baby learns that her cries will evoke a consistent and comforting response from her mother, she develops confidence in her mother as a reliable protector. Her mother becomes her

secure base and she feels comfortable exploring a strange envi
ronment as long as her mother is there. She will be confident in
playing with toys she finds and engaging with other people. She
may check frequently to see where her mother is and at times
move closer to her if she feels her mother is too far away. If something happens to upset her, she will immediately seek her mother's
reassurance. If the mother leaves the room, she will protest and
may cry, even frantically, but will be quickly comforted when the
mother returns and picks her up for a cuddle. She will usually be
able to return to her play quite quickly. There are individual vari-
ations in this. Some babies will need a longer reunion time with
their mothers before they feel comfortable exploring again, and
some may want to sit on her lap and play rather than explore the
room. What is consistent for the baby is the confidence she de-
rives from her relationship with her mother. As she explores her
physical and social world she knows her mother will be there to
protect her.

Tolstoy wrote, "Happy families are all alike; every unhappy
family is unhappy in its own way." In the same vein, babies and
their parents can experience a variety of challenges in forming a
secure attachment, and this can have implications for how the baby
relates to his world as he grows into childhood and adulthood.

In situations where a mother is unable or unwilling to respond
effectively to her baby's signals of distress, the baby has difficulty
developing confidence in having his needs met, and will likely find
other ways to manage the distress he feels. He will learn to suppress his feelings of anxiety and focus his attention on objects he
can play with. Despite feeling distressed and agitated internally,
this baby may show no apparent distress when his mother leaves
the room and will not show noticeable reaction when she returns.
The baby may even actively turn away or avoid contact with his
mother on her return. Because of this lack of reaction, many see

this baby as unusually independent. In fact the baby is putting his energy into avoiding rejection and managing for himself his need for security. This can limit the resources and confidence the baby has to explore his environment and can compromise his approach to learning.

In a relationship where the mother's response to the baby's needs is unpredictable, the baby doesn't experience a consistent response when she is in need of comfort. Sometimes her mother is very responsive and comforts her right away, but at other times when the baby is upset, she doesn't come to her rescue. This leads to ambivalent behaviour on the part of the baby, in which she may be angry and seeking comfort simultaneously. Because her mother does sometimes respond to her when she is upset, she may cry excessively to keep her mother's attention and be fretful and demanding. When her mother leaves the room she will be highly distressed but, unlike the baby who has a secure, predictable attachment, she is not comforted when her mother returns and may be angry or clingy. Because she tends to be frequently anxious, she is often too preoccupied to enjoy her environment and explore new things. This has implications for her experiences with learning.

These patterns of attachment have ramifications for the degree to which a baby relies on emotional and cognitive information and can, therefore, have effects on learning and development. Secure attachment provides a baby with the strongest foundation, in that emotional and cognitive paths of learning are able to work together in a mutually supportive way. Where a baby has received constrained or weak emotional feedback, she has learned to rely more on cognition to understand her world. The baby who has experienced contradictory or unpredictable responses in the past has learned to focus more on emotion than on cognitive approaches to learning. Both of these can be limiting.

The Growth of Attachment

How does attachment grow? Researchers have described the pattern that needs to be repeated over and over: the baby feels hungry and uncomfortable, so she instinctively begins to signal her caregivers. At first, her breathing changes, becoming faster and louder; then she might squirm and make small noises or put her hand in her mouth. If she isn't responded to at this point, she will begin to cry. Somewhere in this gradually escalating pattern of signals, a parent arrives and provides food for the baby, and the discomfort disappears. In the early days and weeks, this pattern will be repeated over and over, not just when the baby is hungry but when she is cold, wet, lying in an uncomfortable position, lonely or frightened.

Soon the parents notice that their daughter stops crying not when she actually gets the first gulp of milk, but as soon as they pick her up. She's begun to recognize that they are the ones who bring the relief from discomfort and pain, and to know that, when they arrive, things will soon be better. She smiles when she sees them, and her parents smile back and another pattern of interaction and communication develops. She learns to trust them to be there when she needs them, and to feel that her attempts to communicate are effective.

The baby has a sense of trust. She feels cared for. This is the beginning of the baby being able to regulate her own emotions. Because she has been consistently and promptly responded to, she is able to stay calm, even when hungry or unhappy. She knows someone will come. She doesn't need to escalate—to cry louder or harder to try to get a response. She doesn't need to try to get extra food this time, or extra attention or extra cuddling, because she knows that there will be more food the next time she's hungry and that comfort and affection will be constant.

If a baby cries and is not responded to, communication, trust, sense of self-efficacy and emotional development all slow down. How long and hard the baby will continue to cry before giving up depends a lot on temperament. The persistent baby will try longer to get someone's attention than the less persistent child will.

At first, babies will smile at almost anyone. As they grow, they become more selective. Then only those close to them get those loving smiles; handed to a stranger the baby will turn his head away or even cry. From the age of about six months, the attachment has become specific.

Developing this attachment and sense of trust takes lots of time. It's built on the hundreds of small interactions between parent and baby that go on every day: the baby in his mother's arms fusses, and she shifts him to a new position; he begins to root and she offers him the breast; after he drinks for a while, he pauses and squirms away, so she lifts him to her shoulder and burps him and so on. Each of the baby's signals brings a response, and those all add up to an attachment relationship. The parent, too, is learning from the baby—learning to understand that when the baby fusses in a particular way it means the baby is hungry, and when the baby squirms or cries in another way it means he's tired. This is not something that can be forged overnight or in a few days or even weeks. Attachment takes time.

The responsive parent provides the baby with a sense of comfort and security. The baby is discovering the answers to important questions. Can people be trusted to meet my needs? Am I understood? Am I loved? Am I an important person? The roots of self-esteem are built here.

This doesn't mean that parents have to be perfect all the time. There will be times when they just can't figure out why the baby is crying, or when the baby wakes up hungry and the mother can't come right away. It's the overall pattern that is important: that most of the time, when the baby is unhappy, the parents respond.

An awareness of the crucial role of attachment to a baby's healthy development helps parents to deal with myths about baby care that persist to this day. I've heard parents who are concerned when their babies cling to them or cry when strangers pick them up, because they think the child is "spoiled" or "too dependent." Teenage mothers sometimes say their baby is "a wimp" because he cries when his mother leaves the room.

While the relationship between a baby and her parents is developing even before she is born, it is about the time she begins to engage in independent movement, usually around six months, that we see a critical phase in the development of a secure attachment that will continue intensely well into the second year. This doesn't mean that a child's need for a secure base ends or diminishes at that point. On the contrary, it is the ongoing reinforcement of the security of that first relationship that guides the formation of relationships with others in the family and social circle. As children grow to school age and into adolescence, the solidity of the home base provided by first relationships is what gives them the confidence to interact competently with their world. They can cope effectively with new experiences when they have the reassurance of a parent who loves them, protects them, comforts them when they are distressed, encourages them to explore and nourishes them emotionally.

In providing this kind of base, parents are recognizing that their children's behaviour grows out of a natural imperative to be attached to the significant people in their lives. Responding to their children's needs does not lead to "clinginess"; it does not encourage a debilitating dependence. Far from it. The child who meets with consistent responsiveness in those closest to him is the child who has an emotionally stable base for exploring his world, learning from new experiences and growing into an autonomous, confident human being. The relationships formed in the first two years of life become an important anchor, a moral touchstone for making decisions and forming judgments. It is crucial that we recognize this role we have in our children's lives and do not underestimate its value. As children's social circles expand, other adults and peers will become influential in their lives, but they cannot and should not replace the central role of parents and primary caregivers. It is through the experiences in the home that children become who they are.

When Attachment Is Compromised

Responding to the feelings, needs and desires of others is at the heart of loving, healthy relationships. In an ideal world, all children would be raised in such a circle of love and nurturance. Sadly, this is not the case. Children can be physically abused and severely neglected, perhaps one of the most severe examples being the experience of children in orphanages that are little more than holding tanks. When attachment occurs at all in such circumstances, it is disorganized, confused and extremely compromising to the child's normal development, emotionally, socially and intellectually. In some orphanage cases, children as old as five have been found to be non-verbal, limited in other forms of communication and suffering from a disrupted capacity to respond to caregivers. [2]

Bleak as this picture is, we can take comfort from the knowledge that, when these children are moved into situations where they receive consistent loving and responsive care, they generally have the resilience to reorganize their attachment behaviour and will begin to thrive physically, emotionally and cognitively. [3] A 1994 study in which low-income mothers exhibiting irritability towards their infants were placed in a program designed to raise maternal responsiveness and sensitivity, demonstrated that the infants, after nine months, were engaging in more sophisticated, exploratory behaviour and showing stronger signs of secure attachment. These benefits were sustained in a follow-up study when the children were three and a half years old.[4] As the child's brain develops, nature collaborates to help undo the damage of early neglect and abuse; however, this is still a far cry from the child's right to receive loving, responsive parenting from the start. Intervention and remediation are costly, and studies of the long-term effects of a poor start in life are comparatively recent and far from conclusive.

As a society what we need to strive for is the creation of circumstances for secure attachments to grow between all parents and their babies. I liken the resulting harmony to having good reception on the radio channel, to being tuned in. If the tuner is off channel, you will be aware of the static all your life.

Attachment in the Roots of Empathy Classroom

John Bowlby, the world-famous psychiatrist and author of classic works on parent–child attachment, wrote, "The more that we can give young people opportunities to meet with and observe *at first hand* how sensitive, caring parents treat their offspring, the more likely are they to follow suit. To learn directly from such parents about the difficulties they meet with and the rewards they obtain, and to discuss with them both their mistakes and their successes are worth, I believe, hundreds of instructional talks."[5]

In our program there is a strong focus on the parent–child attachment relationship. Some programs that teach children about infant care have used a visit by a baby from a nearby daycare centre or even dolls with computer chips that make them cry at unpredictable intervals to expose children to the work of looking after a baby. The children can learn about babies from these experiences, but not the deeper lessons about the relationships they form with those closest to them. When the baby and the parents are in the classroom together, children interact with this vital connection. During successive Roots of Empathy sessions, as the family visits each month, the children are able to watch attachment develop between parents and baby. They are coached to observe how the baby sends cues about his needs to his parents and how the parents attend to those cues. They see how the parents respond to the baby when he is distressed, and they see how the baby comes to prefer the parents to anyone else. They see how the parents become the secure home base to the baby's exploring once he begins to crawl. The children learn quickly how critical it is for the baby's survival and well-being to build this relationship with his parents. In our classes, when the baby is crawling on the blanket and keeps looking back for his mother, we tell the children, "Look, the baby is showing us how important his mother is to him. He needs to know she is there." The children learn to recognize the legitimacy of the baby's feelings and to respect them. That's also another step towards recognizing the legitimacy and value of their own emotions.

It is eleven o'clock on a bright March morning. The sun streaming through the classroom windows shines on the faces of the Grade 2 children sitting around the green blanket. Sophie, at eight months old, is sitting up by herself. When she suddenly starts to cry, the instructor asks, "What does Sophie need now?"

Several children respond, "She needs her mommy." When asked why Sophie needs her mommy right now, the children answer, "Because Sophie knows her mommy is going to look after her." These children know that you can't spoil a baby. Crying is the only language the baby has to let us know that something is wrong.

We tell the children in our program that when a baby cries, it has a problem, and the adults need to figure out what the problem is and help the baby. We emphasize that this isn't always easy, and work with the children to brainstorm about the possible reasons why a baby would cry. Many parents of new babies feel very frustrated as they try to figure out the reason for the baby's unhappiness. Is the baby hungry, tired, wet, bored, too cold, too warm, uncomfortable, in pain, wanting to be held, wanting to be moved, wanting to lie down? There are so many possibilities. In time, though, the parents' efforts to figure all this out begin to pay off, and they can recognize the baby's signals. The baby also gets better at giving precise signals. The behaviours of the baby influence the parents and the behaviours of the parents influence the baby. The Roots of Empathy parents are very candid in sharing with the children the trial-and-error journey they are on as they "learn" their baby. Dr. Ron Barr, a pediatrician and expert on crying gives a reassuring message that we can't always tell why a baby is crying, and that it is normal for babies to have periods of inconsolable crying.

In a Grade 5 class, Anil's mother was answering the children's questions about how she was able to tell what Anil needs when he starts to cry. She told them that the previous Thursday, Anil was crying very loudly and persistently even though she had fed him and changed his diaper. She sang to him, cuddled him, and still he kept crying. Then she noticed that he kept pulling at his ear, and she began to wonder if there was a connection. She took him to the doctor, who diagnosed an ear infection. The children were impressed that a six-month-old baby could so cleverly communicate what the problem was. For the instructor, this is a "teachable" moment—an ideal opportunity to illustrate the language of cues and relationship-building passing between baby and parent. Anil gives his mother a cue, she reads it accurately, helps Anil, and Anil feels comforted and protected. Every time this happens, the connection between Anil and his mother grows stronger and Anil's confidence in how to communicate and be responded to is also strengthened.

Our babies are powerful communicators, right from birth; they tell us what they need. We only need to tune in to their messages. As parents attune to the baby's signals, they are working to make the baby's world understandable to him. They are giving meaning to his cries and he is learning to use them purposefully. With each parental response, the baby is developing a sense of his own competence and a way of managing the stresses he experiences. This dance of attunement is at the core of the baby's healthy sense of self.

While the benefits of secure attachment and attunement are celebrated, children in our program also learn about the implications for a baby when her needs are not met. There is discussion about the effect on the baby when she cries and no one responds. The students learn that eventually the baby will stop crying, but this does not mean that the problem has been resolved. The baby may have fallen silent, but the distress has not disappeared. Inside, she is still upset and anxious. This can be a powerful and validating discussion for children and another bridge to empathy. Many children have at least some experience with being required to "tough it out," to swallow hurt or repress fear. In the context of the baby's experiences, they have an avenue to share experiences about times when their feelings were hurt or they were scared and what would have made it better. The sharing of stories gives children insights about themselves and each other and reinforces how common their feelings are.

Tell the Story of Attachment

When I talk to city officials, I speak of the fact that there is fluoride in our water supply to prevent tooth decay. I tell them we need empathy in the water supply to prevent social decay. When we work on building healthy societies, we should be aware that schools are our water supply. Schools are the place where we can extend the positive influences children receive in their family or create positive influences to combat harmful influences. We have the opportunity to seed civility on a green blanket in the classrooms of the nation.

Older children in the Roots of Empathy classes understand and respect the attachment story. They understand that you can overcome adversity and that you can be confident in defence of what you believe to be right if, from the beginning, you know that you deserve to be loved, trust you will be cared for, and have been shown that you're worth it. It is to our advantage to have the story of human development taught to all children in school; it fosters universal respect for the fundamental importance of secure first relationships and for the family as the most influential source of all that is truly human.

Investing in children during these early years to promote solid, healthy attachments is the best investment a family can make, the best investment a community can make and the best investment the world can make.

EMOTIONAL: LITERACY: THE LANGUAGE OF THE HEART

"When I lost my first tooth, I felt scared. When I lost it, I gave it to my Mom. Then my mother put it in her dresser for safe keepings."

KEYANO, a Grade 2 student in a Roots of Empathy class, describes his emotions about losing his first tooth. It was a scary experience for him and he turned to his mother for help. Keyano describes his mother's solution as a validation for him that this was an important event and that she understood his fear of loss. Keyano is developing a competence that will serve him well all his life. He is acquiring emotional literacy.

Our society prizes print literacy and computer literacy. There is a boom in the tutoring business, and parents are reporting that children as young as Keyano are spending hours each evening on homework assignments just to keep up with an ever-more-demanding curriculum. Our children are exposed to situations that create anxiety about whether they will get the grades to give them access to the "best" high school or university. A parallel trend is the growing isolation of children as they spend increasing periods of time in front of screens, learning the literacy of violence in video games, learning the literacy of insensitivity from TV "reality-shows," or learning the literacy of consumerism from an endless bombardment of advertising. Between these two trends lies a chasm that threatens the spirits of our children. The stress and alienation they are prey to is unprecedented in our history.

While we will always strive, as we should, to support their academic success, we particularly owe it to our children to listen to their hearts, to make sure they have the vocabulary to express their feelings and the absolute confidence that they will be heard with understanding. We owe them the tool of emotional literacy. The wonderful by-product of encouraging our children's emotional literacy is that we as adults stretch emotionally ourselves as we gain invaluable insights into the emotional lives of our children. I see strong parallels between the development of print literacy and the development of emotional literacy.

When, in my parenting programs, I worked with parents to show them the active role they can play in the development of their children's early literacy skills, we talked about how literacy skills are based on communication, relationship and modelling the love of reading. Listening, speaking and relating are skills of expression that come before reading and writing. When it comes to the literacy of feelings, the same order of priority exists. To be able to encourage emotional fluency in our children we need to have developed our own skills in listening, speaking, modelling and relating. In both cases, if we try to take a didactic approach, overriding the relationship and showing disrespect for developmental readiness, we create superficial synaptic connections. This weakens the future structure of the lifelong development of these two literacies rather than building a solid base.

What Is Emotional Literacy?

Emotional literacy is frequently described as the ability to recognize, understand, cope with and express our emotions in appropriate ways. When we add empathy to this mix and put it in the social contexts within which we all live, we have the basis for morally responsible behaviour. It prompts us to speak against injustice, and not only when laws have been broken but also when someone's actions are just plain unfair.

It is a combination of emotional regulation and emotional literacy that allows us to control *how* we express our emotions so that anger can be conveyed without damaging another person; it is emotional literacy that allows us to bring a thoughtful, respectful approach to solving conflicts; and it is emotional literacy that opens the window to empathy, allowing us to see situations from another's perspective and understand their feelings.

The Development of Emotional Literacy

Emotions are an infant's first language and it is a universal language. Of all the literacies of childhood, emotional literacy is the foundational one. In one well-known experiment, one-year-old babies were placed on a table with a clear sheet of Plexiglass laid flat to join the table with another one. The baby's mother would be at the other side. In each case, the baby would crawl towards the edge of the first table and look at the glass. It looked as though there was nothing in between—the baby could clearly see the floor several feet below. And yet there was a hard surface. Should the baby keep crawling or should he stop?

Researchers looked at the impact on the baby of his mother's reaction. Invariably the baby would look to his mother. If her expression showed happiness and encouragement, fourteen out of the nineteen babies in the experiment crawled across the glass to the other table. If, on the other hand, the baby's mother looked frightened or worried, her baby stopped at the edge of the first table. [I]

Powerful messages were conveyed, without a word or a gesture, just by the expression on the mother's face. Pre-verbal emotional literacy is emotional communication in its purest form; a baby can't be tricked or misled by a thicket of words. He surrenders complete trust to his parent, creating a bond that would support a cable car.

We have seen in our exploration of attachment that, from earliest infancy, children have the capacity to communicate feelings to their caregivers. This communication happens through behaviour that includes crying, facial expressions, vocalizations and other physical signals, all of which produce reciprocal responses from the caregivers. A rich emotional tapestry is created, and even before a child learns to speak she becomes adept at giving and receiving non-verbal cues. This is the earliest phase of emotional literacy—expressing feelings of joy or anger or distress, then experiencing responses that soothe and comfort, and as a result of consistent response, learning to regulate the intensity of feelings.

This non-verbal communication is not supplanted by verbal communication as a child learns to talk, but becomes an integral part of his communication system. We continue to communicate as much through facial expressions and body language as we do through the words we use. As children move into situations such as child care or school, where social interactions with children and adults outside the family are required, their skills in using and reading non-verbal cues become increasingly important. The practice they have had in the family enables them to understand and respond better to the behaviour of others even when those others are not articulating their wishes, feelings or intentions in words. The ability to read and respond to these cues is key to the development of social competence. Just as a child can't sing along with the group when she doesn't know the words to the song, children who don't have the vocabulary to express feelings cannot participate effectively in social contexts.

As language skills develop, preschoolers learn to use words in addition to—or instead of—actions to convey what they want or what they feel. In the Roots of Empathy classroom the children see the baby pulling Mommy's hair. Mommy says, "Ow! That hurts!" and gently disentangles the baby's fingers from her hair. She doesn't get mad at the baby. She understands that the baby didn't intend to hurt her. When the children witness this and discuss what happened, they are able to explore the idea of the intentions connected to actions. The baby loves his mommy. In grabbing her hair, his intention is to get closer to her, to have more physical contact with her. The mother's gentle response recognizes the love behind the baby's actions. The discussion gives the children the opportunity to talk about the difference it can make to how you react to someone's action when you take the time to think about what their intentions might be.

A further stage in emotional understanding occurs when children begin to connect ideas and feelings—"I am sad because I left my teddy at home." This connection between cause and effect is the basis for logical thinking. In one of the exercises used in our program, children are given a picture of a girl who is sad and asked to reflect on reasons she might be feeling that way. Answers range from "She's upset because other kids are teasing her" to "She's sad because her dad just lost his job." The deepest learning always has an emotional component. The emotions help us remember and help us connect one piece of knowledge to the other pieces of information already stored in our brains.

It takes a combination of skill in reading non-verbal cues, insight into one's own feelings, ability to express them, and awareness of the emotions and intentions of others to equip children with the social and emotional competence they will need to function well in school and in life. The practical work children do in the Roots of Empathy classroom gives them the concrete experience that builds these skills. It may be writing a letter to the baby, starting with the words "The important thing about me is . . ." or it may be group work during which children discuss the range of feelings a student might experience if she were new to the school ("shy, shivery, excited, happy to make a friend"). In their book *The Irreducible Needs of Children*, T. Berry Brazelton, a renowned pediatrician, and Stanley Greenspan, an influential child psychiatrist, have this to say about the importance of well-developed emotional and social skills for school-aged children: "To negotiate the intricacies of multiple relationships within a group, they have to reason on a very sophisticated level. . . This ability to diagnose group dynamics helps children to develop cognitive and social skills that will be very valuable in school—and beyond school, in the real world. They learn that most of life operates in shades of gray, not in all-or-nothing extremes. Sizing up these subtle shades of gray requires understanding that feelings can exist in relative terms."[2]

Emotional Literacy in the Roots of Empathy Classroom

Emotional literacy can only develop in an environment where children feel safe or supported. When they feel criticized, ridiculed or not respected, they are at risk of shutting down any expression of emotion and eventually their internal awareness of their feelings may also be compromised. One of the ways our program teaches children the importance of this internal awareness occurs in classes when the baby is being fed and has reached satiation point. We ask them how they can tell that the baby has had enough. There is a chorus of responses: "She turned her head sideways." "She pushed the spoon away." "She shut her mouth tight." "She's spitting the food out." Agreeing with all these responses, we emphasize that the baby knows better than anyone when she has had enough, and that if we don't pay attention to this, if we override the baby's judgment, she will lose her sense of certainty about when she has had enough to eat. When we deny children the right to their feelings, such as when we repeatedly tell a child "there's nothing to be sad about" instead of acknowledging the sadness, she will stop sharing her feelings. The feelings will go underground, communication is thwarted, and the child's ability to seek out solutions to the problems that led to her fear is blocked. It is like living in an oppressive environment where you can't speak the language or aren't allowed to practice your religion.

In one Roots of Empathy kindergarten class where the instructor talked about emotions during the first session, Ramon, who had always sat huddled in the corner during the lesson, perked up for the first time. When the instructor said "Feelings are not wrong, they are your feelings and it is okay to feel that way— whether you are sad or angry, scared or happy," Ramon made eye contact with the instructor and moved up to join the group. That was the beginning of his involvement and lively participation in the class. One of the activities that helps to create greater awareness of feelings is taking an "emotional barometer" reading of the class. The children choose a sticker that reflects how they are feeling: a red sticker for feeling good, a green sticker for so-so, and a blue sticker for not so good. The children then put them on a big sheet of graph paper so that they can see how the whole class is feeling. It encourages children to reflect on how they are feeling themselves, makes them aware that other children may not be having such a good day, and shows how our feelings can fluctuate.

In one of our classes a child with special needs who had great difficulty with most academic subjects became excited when the instructor began to discuss emotions. Although Courtney could not keep up with the others when it came to reading and math, she understood emotions and recognized them in herself and others. For the first time she was able to participate fully with the rest of the class, and it was a vivid demonstration to the other students of the universality of emotions. This experience is borne out by research in other situations involving curriculum that deals with the vocabulary of feelings and the management of emotions. The children concerned were from regular and special education classrooms. Results showed that the children "increased their verbal fluency in labelling and discussing their emotions and the children in the special education classes may have made pro-portionately greater gains than the regular education children in learning how to manage their emotions."[3] It was also argued that the curriculum helped the children develop further interpersonal problem-solving skills and behavioural self-control because of enhanced awareness of their own emotion processes and their ability to think about them.

In our program we teach the children that babies have intense emotions from the moment of birth, and that they express these emotions through various signals—including crying. Babies are the best teachers of emotional literacy because their emotions are not disguised in any way. When the baby visits the classroom with her family, the students are given unique opportunities to study the unfolding of emotions. They learn to detect emotions of surprise, interest or boredom as they observe the baby's raised eyebrows, rate of breathing or staring, unblinking eyes.

Jamal is lying on his tummy on the blanket, and the instructor places a ball in front of him. The ball is transparent with a colourful patterned disc rotating inside. Jamal reaches out towards the ball and his hand knocks it, causing it to roll out of his reach. He struggles towards it and again the ball rolls away when he touches it. After several unsuccessful attempts to grasp the ball, Jamal scrunches up his face, his legs go rigid and he starts to scream. The instructor asks the Grade 2 class, "What do you think Jamal is feeling now?" Shannon says, "He's sad because he can't get the ball." Jack calls out, "I think he's really mad." Another child shyly offers, "Maybe Jamal is just frustrated." As Jamal's mother picks him up and places the ball between his hands, the lively discussion continues. The children relate Jamal's behaviour to his temperament. He was not easily distracted from his interest in the ball, and he was very persistent in trying to reach it. They are equally clear that his crying is not an indication that he is a "bad" baby. They are integrating what they observe with the themes they have been exploring.

This scene will be discussed the following week when Jamal and his mother are not due to visit. Recalling Jamal's reactions leads the class to talk about his attachment to his mother. The instructor asks, "When Jamal was frustrated, did he look to his mom for help?" There is also lots of scope to discuss the temperament traits of intensity, perseverance and distractibility. The children give examples from their own experience: learning to read, to skip, to ride a two-wheeler, to overcome difficulties with math. Now that there is some distance from the events, they are able to reflect on the frustration they felt and how they overcame it. They explore what caused the feeling. Were they able to talk about it with someone else? What made the situation better? As they relate their observations of the baby's behaviour to their own experiences, students are given the words for emotions and an opportunity to use them. They learn to express feelings: "I feel hurt when other kids don't ask me to play with them." In the trust established in the Roots of Empathy classroom, students respond with understanding and generosity to these statements, telling the boy who felt hurt that "You can always play with us." To create awareness in children of how their classmates are feeling will build an empathic awareness beyond the classroom.

Embarrassment is a feeling that all children have experienced at some time. Children in our classes are coached not to cause embarrassment to the mother when she breastfeeds the baby in class, and not to laugh if the baby soils his diaper. The caring relationship the children build up with the Roots of Empathy family ensures that this coaching is taken to heart. The topic of embarrassment is explored further in small group discussions in which students respond to various scenarios. These are "what if" situations that allow children to reveal emotions safely through creating a collective group response to questions such as "How would a person feel if. . ?" or "What could someone do to help them out?" They can hear what their buddies think and contribute their own thoughts. The experience of feeling different—sometimes contradictory— emotions at the same time is also explored. In response to the question "If your friend made a mistake, how do you think he would feel?" children in Grades 3 and 4 come up with multiple emotions. "He'd be shy, unhappy, nervous." They have clearly tried to immerse themselves in the emotions of the situation presented to them. Research reported by Carolyn Saarni, a developmental psychologist and researcher on children's emotional competence, has shown that by age eight, children can put together as many as four separate emotions in response to the same situation, including a different level of intensity of each distinct emotion.[4]

In our program, the process for exploring emotion is collective and collaborative, and the result is the building of human connection among the students. In much the same way second language skills are taught in school, by creating opportunities for students to use the language in meaningful contexts we give children an opportunity to use their language of emotions and to hear how others use the language. This gives them fluency and greatly increases their empathy as they learn to understand how others feel.

In all of these situations, students are following key steps to emotional literacy:

- observing the baby's experiences and the emotions they inspire
- naming the emotions
- anchoring the emotion in themselves privately through discussion, reflection, art and journalling
- discussing their feelings with others

In the classroom the children share the common experience of watching the baby and hearing the mother, the instructor and the other students talk about what they observe and how it relates to what the baby is feeling. The learning of emotional literacy in the Roots of Empathy class is so effective because it is based on the experiential learning from the baby.

Many communities now have breakfast programs or subsidized lunch programs for children. They've recognized something that should be obvious: you can't teach a hungry child. But it is equally true that you can't teach a sad child, a worried child or a frightened child. Teachers have commented on the unique opportunity the Roots of Empathy program gives them to observe their students from a different perspective as they interact with the baby and with the instructor. The emotional toll of struggles at home or in the playground often emerges, providing insights into classroom behaviour. The statement "I felt sad when the ambulance took my mom to the hospital, but I couldn't tell anyone" gives a Grade 3 teacher an entirely fresh perspective on a small boy's apparently angry and disruptive behaviour. In this case the child's mother was suffering from depression and had attempted suicide, and other family members warned him not to talk about it. Children's behaviour is reflective of how they feel. An aware teacher now has the opportunity to use interventions that respond to a child's real emotions and understand behaviour that might otherwise have drawn only disapproval or punishment.

When we respond only to behaviour, without paying attention to the underlying feelings and motivations for that behaviour, it can be said that we are responding at the moral reasoning level of a small child. Ask a three-year-old whether it is worse to break twenty plates by accident or one plate on purpose, and the pre-schooler will probably say "twenty plates." At this stage they are responding to the result of the action, not the intention behind it. We can translate this into the world of the "zero tolerance" policies that have been instituted in many school systems. Such policies, which impose automatic penalties for narrowly defined infractions, tend to look at the result of an action, and not the cause or intention. So the child who brought in a butter knife to slice his frozen bagel at lunchtime is suspended for "carrying a dangerous weapon." A boy who defends himself when attacked by three other boys is given a detention for "being involved in a fight." A girl is given a week of detentions for threatening another girl, but in fact she was confronting someone who was threatening to beat up her little brother who was in Grade 1. To children, this kind of policy feels unjust and they feel betrayed by—and in some cases contemptuous of—the adults who are supposed to understand and protect them. They see violations of the moral understanding that we are hoping to foster in them.

The Capacity to Care and the Capacity to Think

Many would argue that taking time to teach emotional literacy and empathy in schools is time stolen from teaching academic skills and developing cognitive aptitude. This view is simply not supported by research. In fact, there is a strong connection between understanding of emotion and cognitive ability. Experiencing an emotion by its very nature requires cognitive skills. To arouse your nervous system, you have to be aware that something has changed in your environment and be able to understand and interpret its implications for you. We do this every day, some of us more skilfully than others.

Studies show that students involved in programs designed to increase empathy have stronger scores in higher-order reading comprehension than comparison students.[5] Other studies have confirmed that training in empathy enhances both critical skills and creative thinking. The gains are not simply in moral reasoning, but in the ability to reason generally. The process of demonstrating empathy is linked to skills such as insight, problem-solving, and cognitive and personal flexibility.[6]

We have to question the value of intellectual achievement that is not allied with emotional literacy. Who has not had the experience of being bombarded with the weight of someone's expertise in a particular field of knowledge, while being denied any acknowledgement that the "expert" sees his captive audience as human beings with their own questions and opinions? What can be learned in an environment where our emotional responses are ignored? In my view, not much. When the heart is engaged as actively as the mind, we have created the conditions for deep and lasting learning.

Empathy helps us to find our moral compass in a world where we are at risk of being anaesthetized by sensory and information overload. It brings us back to the fundamental importance of what it is to be human, what it is to truly see another's joy or sadness or pain. Emotional literacy gives us the tools to take these innermost feelings and beliefs and give them voice. In Roots of Empathy, the world's youngest teachers demonstrate emotion in its pure state and draw us back to simple yet deep levels of connection. In hundreds of classrooms, babies are teaching students that it is cool to care.

9

AUTHENTIC: COMMUNICATION: SPEAKING FROM THE HEART

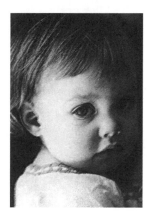

Child-led Conversations

IN THE WORK I DO training professionals involved in the field of parenting and family literacy, or child care, I use this "Baby Glances" picture and a number of other pictures from my series "Picture Talks" to illustrate authentic communication. The picture is used as a springboard for dialogue between the adult—be it parent, caregiver or teacher—and the preschooler, in which the child's imagination directs where the conversation will go. There are no right or wrong answers, and the adult's contributions to the dialogue serve to validate and encourage the child's observations. There are no phony attempts to get the child to answer a question to which the adult obviously already has the answer. In the example I have given, I suggest that the adult might prompt discussion by saying:

- Tell me about this picture.
- How do you think the baby feels?
- If the baby could talk, what do you think she would say?
- What would you say to the baby?

This approach allows the child to take the lead and direct the conversation to what appeals to him. Through the invitation to the child to talk about the picture, the adult gains insight into the child's perspective, building the adult's empathy for the child and forging a closer connection in the communication circle. I encourage the adult to share in the conversation as well, by revealing the thoughts, ideas and memories the picture inspires for her. This enhances the authenticity of the communication as the genuine thoughts and ideas of the adult are shared in a mutual, playful, respectful way with the child. The discussion leads to the adult and child learning as much about each other as about the topic inspired by the picture.

The way the family communicates not only determines how a child develops literacy but also gives the child their view of the world. Parents connect the dots for their children; because they know the child's prior experience, they can build on what is already meaningful for the child, giving sense to the language used. This works and enriches learning in ways that isolated instruction never can. When a parent says, "The lady on the bus has white hair like Grandma," this conjures up real pictures for the child and the connections are real. Relationships teach the child.

Why is this important? Children develop social and emotional competence through the quality of the relationships they first develop with parents and those closest to them. What we say to them is important, but more crucial still is how we say it and what we are conveying about our respect for them as individuals. Brazelton and Greenspan express it well: "Empathy is taught not by telling children to be nice to others or to try to understand others, but by parents' having the patience to listen to children and children's feeling understood. Once they understand what empathy feels like, they can create it in their relationships."[1]

In the model of authentic communication I advocate, where the adult is following the lead taken by the child, we are also encouraging the child's sense of her valued self, where her ideas are interesting and her perspective has validity. This helps the child build a core of sustainable self-esteem, an inner moral sense that will stand up to the challenges that are an inevitable part of growing into adulthood. If children have a learned method for deciding, for making judgments, if they have internalized principles to live by, things that feel true for them, they have the armour they need to say no to things that make them feel uncomfortable or strike them as wrong. In a way it is like using formulae in math. We don't have to start from scratch every time; we can use the pattern, and we won't get the wrong answer if we use the right formula.

Threats to Authentic Communication

Authentic communication takes time and focus and active awareness. These are commodities in short supply in the busy technology-driven world we inhabit today. The percentage of parents in the workforce, be they single parents or partners in a dual-parent family, is higher than ever before. What does the day look like? There's a rush to get out the door in the morning, drop children off at school or daycare, rush to work through traffic snarls, put in an intense day on the job, face the evening commute, pick up kids, prepare evening meals, deal with homework (your own and your child's), bath-time, bedtime, bedtime story, collapse! Where in the midst of all this is there time for real talk? And I haven't even mentioned "screen-time."

Around the world children are spending increasing amounts of time in front of television, computer and video screens. The average length of time has variously been reported as from three to six hours per day. A news release for a 1999 Kaiser Foundation (U.S.) study on "Kids & Media @ The New Millennium" blazed out the headline: "KIDS SPEND EQUIVALENT OF FULL WORK WEEK USING MEDIA." The article included alarming statistics about the high percentage of children aged eight and older with a TV in their bedroom (65 per cent) and the low percentage of parents who watched TV with their children (19 per cent where the children were under eight years of age and 5 per cent where children were eight years or older). [2] What is being lost here? What is not happening while children are engaged for the equivalent of an adult's work week in front of the various screens in our homes?

Family conversations are happening less and less. Family dinner, an ideal time for talking over the events of the day and sharing news about everyone's "highs" and "lows," is disappearing or takes place distractedly within sight or sound of a television program. Games have become a solitary electronic pursuit instead of a lively exchange among siblings and parents. Even the time a child has for unstructured daydreaming and allowing her imagination to roam free is being eroded.

Communication between parents and children is being whittled away to blocks of a few minutes each day. And sadly, the pace of life often results in these communications turning into staccato directions or instructions—"Come here. Brush your teeth. Wash your hands"—on the part of parents, and minimal requests—"Can I have a drink? Can I go outside? Where is my backpack?"—from the children. While these are part of the necessary exchanges of family life, by themselves they are hardly what most of us would consider to be communication.

Parent and child interactions can sound more like interrogations than conversations.

"Who broke the glass?"
"I don't know."
"Well, you and I are the only ones here, so it must have been you."
"Why did you ask me if you already knew?"

We need to find another way. We need to restore our blocks of family time with no agenda.

The Strength of Authentic Communication

Real communication happens at an emotional level. When we share our feelings, opinions, values and deeply held beliefs with one another, we are able to relate as human beings. Authentic communication is supportive to the growth of social and emotional competence and a basis for developing empathy. Yet for many of us the challenge of putting ourselves into the dialogue as an equal and respectful partner can be very unsettling. Children love to hear stories of their parents' lives and experiences, as long as the stories are not of the "I had to walk six miles to school, uphill both ways" genre. They want to hear stories that make us human. We need to tell our stories as honestly as we can, making the feelings that inhabit them come alive. Children like to know about the challenges and tough times too. It makes their own challenges a little easier to face.

One of the things we often feel we should not do is let our children see us cry. Parents are often afraid that if children see them cry or know that they are unhappy, they will feel insecure or afraid because their parents seem weak. But children always know when their parents are unhappy. They don't need to see our tears to know that something is wrong. If we then keep the reason for that unhappiness a secret, our child's imagination will create its own frightening and disturbing possibilities. Perhaps, the child thinks, this is my fault. Perhaps I have done something to make Daddy sad. Or perhaps it's something so terrible that Daddy can't tell me.

Never seeing adults cry or express their sadness also gives children unreasonable expectations that they may carry into their own adult lives. If their experience has been that adults are never sad but always cheerful in the face of any situation, what role model does the young adult have to follow when he's feeling devastated by the breakup of a relationship or a disappointment at work? All he can do is hide his emotions, and so the pattern continues into yet another generation.

Imagine a mother chatting with a friend while holding her nine-month-old baby in her arms. The baby notices some children run past the window and tries to get her mother's attention. She makes "uh, uh" sounds and gestures with her arms towards the window. If the mother is not attuned to her baby's cues, she may be irritated by the baby's interruption of her conversation and turn the baby away from the window. In doing this she has lost an opportunity for communication and connection. The baby, like all babies, needs to experience a sense of efficacy, learn that they can connect to the important people in their lives and make things happen.

The idea of following the baby's lead and interests is a significant factor in the development of children who are curious observers and good communicators, and who will share what they find interesting with family and friends. If the mother described above is usually attentive to her baby's cues, an isolated incident like this one won't do any harm to the baby's developing sense of self or her attachment to learning, but if this is more the norm than not, it could present difficulties for the baby's optimal development. It is the communication system of the family, the responses of the parents or caregivers, that reinforces the baby's fascination with life and creates a fearless learner.

If the mother, still talking with her friend, carries the baby over to the window and shares in the baby's interest and excitement about the children going past, then she is offering a responsiveness that enhances the baby's sense of self. Some might say this is "spoiling" the baby, catering to her every whim. But it is important to look at what is being built here. This is how a child develops social competence, the ability to communicate with and receive responses from another human being, even when she has only sounds and gestures to make it happen. Secure attachments result from satisfactorily meshing needs and communication between the baby and the parents. This is what sets the child on the path to becoming a successful partner in a working relationship.

Now let's imagine that a Grade 4 teacher is in the middle of a math lesson when suddenly a boy—a little boy who never seems to be on the same page as everyone else and who is always easily distracted—raises his hand and waves it wildly. She asks him what he wants and he announces, "Miss, it's started snowing!" If she is not open to responding to such moments, she might say, "Jamie, why don't you ever pay attention? We're doing math right now."

Another reaction, one that does not pour cold water on a child's natural excitement, might be: "Jamie, thank you for pointing that out. What will you play at recess now there's snow on the ground?" Or, even better: "Class, Jamie's just noticed that it's snowing, so we might need our snowpants on at recess. Thank you, Jamie." Those comments raise Jamie's status in the eyes of every child in the class. And Jamie, knowing that he's been heard and respected, has a stronger motivation for reconnecting to the lesson, and is likely to pay attention better and be a more engaged learner the rest of the day.

These are deceptively simple examples of capitalizing on special moments to communicate on an authentic level. The child initiates the exchange and the adult goes to where the child is, steps into his shoes to understand what is interesting from the child's point of view, and responds from this perspective. The child's excitement of discovery is not lost in the adult's busy schedule. We can always find opportunities to give our children the starring role they deserve.

Through authentic communication we can model values of inclusion. Talk to your children about the times when you felt left out as a child and the times when you feel left out now. The joy of being sought after for the relay race because you were a fast runner. What kind of awkwardness or feelings of being left out did you feel when you were the last girl in your class to get your period? Or did you feel humiliated because all your friends grew six inches over the summer and you were the "shrimp" of the group in September? Parents who share vulnerability share emotional memory. You are communicating a great deal about the justice of social inclusion and the needless pain caused by exclusion. At the same time, your children are experiencing a genuine sense of the human beings their parents are. In such contexts, you are building communication with your child that will weather the challenges to communication often brought with adolescence.

We can take opportunities to discuss with our children all kinds of examples of unfair or unkind treatment of people, and focus on the emotions of the people involved. There are probably many stories from our own lives to share. But there are also examples in the newspaper and on the television every day that can be springboards to discussion. In a 1994 survey of children aged eleven to sixteen, conducted by Children Now, a U.S. advocacy group on policies affecting children, a high percentage of children said they felt angry or sad or depressed after watching the news.[3] There is obviously a real need to connect with our children about what is going on in the world and their relationship to it.

Children also need to know that we enjoy them and their presence in our lives. In my work with parents I have been privileged to hear: "You have given me permission to enjoy my children!" It's hard to find pleasure in parenting when our focus is on making children obey and follow the rules, but when we can relax and share ourselves with our children, everyone's sense of enjoyment is enhanced.

When we show our children that we value what they have to say, and when we respond with honesty, we are communicating authentically. The rewards, in terms of raising children with levels of social and emotional competence that can make their lives rich in relationships will show even in the next generation.

Authentic Communication in the Roots of Empathy Classroom

In the Roots of Empathy program, parents and instructors speak to children honestly and share with them their real thoughts and emotions. In one class the instructor was talking with the students about bullying. She grew up in the only black family in a white neighbourhood and she shared with the class the bullying and name-calling, much of it racist, that she experienced as a child. She began to list the names she'd been called, and suddenly felt overwhelmed with emotion and began to cry. Tears welled up in the classroom teacher's eyes as well. The students looked at them in awe. They'd never seen either of these women cry before. This was a very powerful moment for them. What the students saw in that moment was how the actions of children, who were about their age at the time, continued to have a profound effect on an adult woman, their instructor, and that their teacher so empathized with this story from her colleague's childhood that she wept too. The pain caused by bullying lasts much longer than the few minutes it takes to say the words.

The classroom discussion that ensued was powerful because that instructor was willing to communicate authentically with the children. She was willing to trust and respect the children, sharing experiences and emotions that were important to her on the deepest level.

In another class, the mother, who was about thirty years old, talked very frankly with the class about her experiences as a new parent. Her baby was colicky. He cried a lot, and she had trouble breast-feeding—she felt she couldn't comfort him. She told the students, "If I had had my son at eighteen, there's a strong chance I might have hurt him. But because I had him when I was older, I planned for him. I have a partner who loves me and is good with him. I have a helpful mother-in-law. I can have a latte with my best friend every day if I want to. I have a lot of people to support me. With all that, there isn't a day goes by that I don't cry when my baby cries inconsolably; I feel helpless. I feel lucky that I have so much support to help me deal with the tough times. I feel compassion for young parents who may end up hurting their babies because they have no one to help them out." This candid revelation had a deep emotional impact on the students. Ideas delivered with an emotional component have a longer life. They enter at the cellular, not just the cognitive level. When the students talked about parenting at the end of the year, they all said things like "Never shake a baby" and "Have a plan." In our program we make a lot of space for dialogue, for sharing views, whether it is child to child, child to adult, or adult to child. This dialogue helps children to inform themselves about who they are, and what values are important. This is a tremendously important defence against risky behaviour.

The Roots of Empathy program is one of relationships. It is built on human interaction, starting with the dance of attunement between mother and baby that unfolds on the green blanket in the classroom. It continues in the sense of family that builds up between the students and the baby. It extends into the community that is built among the students as the school year progresses and as they learn what it takes to raise a human being, and just as importantly, what it takes to be a human being. The extent to which this evolution is accomplished would not be possible without the authentic communication that permeates every encounter, or without our baby, who keeps everyone honest.

Everyone involved in the program has stories to tell about thrilling moments and tender moments. The baby's achievements are instantly recognized as cause for celebration. As I recounted earlier, when a baby rolled over for the very first time during a classroom visit, the instructor said that all conversation immediately stopped. The class stared at the baby, who had been on her tummy and was now on her back. They spontaneously began to applaud and cheer. The instructor said it was like being at a hockey game where someone had just scored a goal!

During one of the Roots of Empathy family visits, the class was discussing emotions. The baby's mother explained to the class her feelings about the surgery the baby had recently undergone to repair her cleft palate. The mother told the class that with the corrective surgery or without it, her child would always be a beautiful baby to her. Her words communicated to the children the intrinsic worth of a human being; she showed how the lens of motherhood can make every child unconditionally lovable. This resulted in children asking their parents questions like "Would you love me if I was blind?" or "Would you love me if I failed?" As a result of the family classroom visits, the children often connected more closely with their own families. For these students, the mother's ability to communicate her love in words as well as deeds was a model for them of the value of unguarded emotional forthrightness. Her trust in the relationships built up in the classroom made it easier to say to these ten-year-olds what she might be too inhibited to say among her peers.

When we study our Communication theme, we have an activity involving the use of American Sign Language which teaches children a great deal about the kind of real communication that can happen even when you cannot use spoken words. We separate the children into small groups, and give each group different sign-language words. Then they are asked to teach everybody in the class what their word means. This process of communicating as a group to a bigger group allows children to experience the frustration of not being understood, and collaborating to be effective. They gain respect for difference through the example of those who can't hear.

When it comes to larger societal issues and their root causes, even very young children can surprise you with their depth of understanding and ability to share meaningful insights. In our classes, we teach the children to sing the old lullaby "Rockabye, Baby," which has the line "When the bough breaks, the cradle will fall." We ask the students, "In real life, what could make the cradle fall?" The children's answers are remarkably consistent: Poverty. Daddy losing his job. War. Racism. Children demonstrate an acute awareness of social issues and in particular their impact on families. Some of the most poignant artwork that has emerged from our program was created by students deeply affected by the events of September 11, 2001.

A Roots of Empathy instructor told me about his experience in a kindergarten class. One little girl, Tara, edged her way to his side every time he visited, and rested her head on his knee and patted

Roots of Empathy helps children to understand what it feels like to be left out.
This empathic little boy showed us a profile of social inclusion: he included
a classmate isolated in the playground. Without empathy we
cannot get to conflict resolution or altruism.

I felt proud when my baby sister Sarah was born.

LEFT: This girl understood the concept of intrinsic pride taught in Roots of Empathy. To her, pride was private—not like medals, ribbons and trophies that mark publicly acknowledged achievements. Her pride of family gave her an anchor that did not depend on any external comparison of ability. It defined who she was and allowed her to be happy, independent of the evaluation of others.

BELOW: Six-year-old Michelle drew her pain with aching clarity. The acid of name-calling corrodes children's self-esteem and crushes their spirit. Through the Roots of Empathy program children gain insight into the feelings of others and become less likely to hurt one another.

Michelle I cry Because My friend. hurt My feelings.

David may have been only six years old and unable to print "people are shouting," but he understood the impact of witnessing domestic violence first-hand. Children in the Roots of Empathy program become advocates for babies. David brilliantly captured the metaphor of home by drawing a simple window.

Ricky had imperfect spelling but perfect emotional pitch. He was attuned to his friend's emotional state. How unfortunate that in life we seldom measure what constitutes humanity. Children in Roots of Empathy are encouraged to see themselves as "changers"—people that have the ability to challenge what is not fair and to help those with problems. Every classroom, playground, neighbourhood and community needs more Rickys.

In Roots of Empathy classrooms, solidarity is built when children share their feelings of vulnerability, talking about what makes them nervous or frightened. Nirmala may have misheard "honour role" but was clearly on a roll.

Maddy acknowledged a personal milestone she reached with the backing of her dad. The celebration of the Roots of Empathy's baby's milestones encourages discussion about children's own milestones.

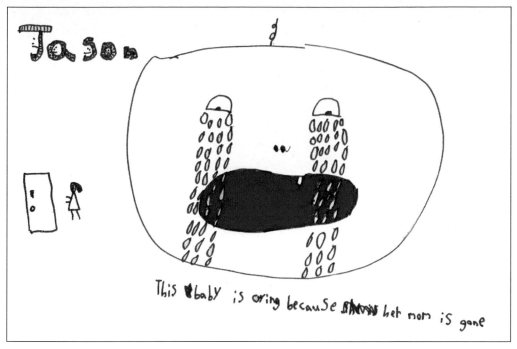

This baby is crying because her mom is gone

ABOVE: When children understand that babies cry for social and emotional reasons, that understanding works to prevent future child abuse. Jason demonstrated the cognitive aspect of empathy; he understood that babies can feel lonely.

LEFT: This little boy's personal "trail of tears" and his ability to explain his sadness allowed other children in his class to understand the impact of bullying. The courage required to share humiliation is always respected in Roots of Empathy classrooms.

I was builbied when a boy in grade 6 pushed me down in the snow and i felt sad. I started crying.

I am proud becaus I cheer my friend up becaus kids are makeing fun of her skin colour.

Our little hero in this picture understood the impact of racism. As Ursula Franklin says, peace is not just the absence of war but the presence of justice and the absence of fear. Roots of Empathy seeds peace in the hearts of children so that they can seed it in the playgrounds. This little girl is changing the world.

Try not to get mad at a baby because thay might learn to be mean when thay grow up.

Try not to get mad at a baby because thay might learn to be mean when thay grow up.

Roots of Empathy attempts to break intergenerational cycles of violence and poor parenting. This little boy understood. He graphically demonstrated the vulnerability of a baby and the power of parents not just physically, but in the formation of character and predisposition to "meanness."

The classrooms of the country are a microcosm of society. Roots of Empathy uses art as a vehicle to draw out the poetry in children. Children never draw what they see; they draw what they feel. In their art they speak to themselves not to an audience. Their work is a pure rendering of their emotional state and thinking at any given time. Children will put in their line drawings what they cannot say with words. For them, drawing is a reflective and healing medium. Teachers seldom know the personal horrors that children harbour as they sit at their desks in the classroom. Many children weather private wars of abuse and neglect in their lives. Art in Roots of Empathy classes creates a bridge from student to student and from student to teacher, enabling them to empathize and open a dialogue.

They are chasing me I told Them To stop.

NO WAR!

ABOVE: For many children recess is a time of fear. In her Roots of Empathy class, Fanstina recalled a time when she was afraid and was not helped. The powerful image this little girl drew is reminiscent of Edvard Munch's painting *The Scream*. Roots of Empathy creates safe and caring schools where every child feels empowered to challenge cruelty and to help a friend in trouble.

LEFT: In the theme Who Am I?, Roots of Empathy students reflect on the kind of world they would wish for their baby to grow up in. Most children say they want a peaceful world. There will be no peace until we are able to build on our shared experiences and see beyond our differences.

his leg as he read to the group or talked. Later in the program, the instructor asked the children to draw a picture of their favourite "Roots" moment. Thirty-one children wrote that they liked it best when the baby smiled, or crawled or laughed. Tara wrote that she liked it best when the baby was sad. When the instructor asked her about it, she said that when the baby was sad, the baby was like her. Tara felt sad all the time. Conversations don't get more authentic than that.

Authentic Communication, Authentic Growth

One of the most important tools we have in getting relationships right is authentic communication, whether it is the first all-important relationship between child and parent or the relationships we make as we grow. We have to listen with attunement and we have to be prepared to respond with openness.

There are pockets of time in every day that belong to our children. When these moments happen, we need to clear our minds of the adult agenda and focus our attention on being with them. The stories I have told in this chapter demonstrate that how the child learns and views his competence has everything to do with the quality of the communication we share at these times. The respect we convey to the child in our words, gestures and facial expressions is internalized, and evolves into a strong sense of self and competence that endures.

10

SOCIAL INCLUSION: SETTING A PLACE FOR EVERYONE

Stop racism and we will all live in a better world.

W HEN WE INTERVIEWED Dr. Robert Glossop of the Vanier Institute of the Family for our Roots of Empathy newsletter, he commented, "There are two kinds of social capital. There is a bonding type, which is to feel closely affiliated with those who are like you, and there is the bridging type of social capital, which is to feel closely affiliated with those who are different from you. In our society, when there is increasing diversity by virtue of heritage, race, culture, religion, language and so on, whatever we can do to give people an opportunity to experience not only how we differ from one another but what we hold in common is a vital contribution."[1]

Diversity Enriches Our Experience

In the Roots of Empathy program, celebration of our differences and recognition of the common ground that binds us together as human beings are used to teach the value of social inclusion. We talk about "setting a place at the table for everybody." Whether a person's seat at the table is in a wheelchair, a rocking chair or a high chair.

During an early family visit to one of our classes, baby Manu arrived with all his thick, dark hair shaved off. He looked so different! The children—this was a Grade 2 class—naturally began to ask, "What happened to Manu's hair?" One little boy eagerly spoke up, telling them, "I know, I know! It's because we are special, and in our religion the baby gets his hair all shaved off when he's two months old. It's because we're Tamil, and I'm Tamil just like Manu!"

In another class, as the mother sang a lullaby to her baby in Spanish, a little girl beamed because it was the same song, in the same language, that her own mother had sung to her when she was a baby. The experience validated her heritage, to her and in the eyes of her classmates. Under what other circumstances would she have been able to hear songs in Spanish, beyond her own family and outside of her community culture? How many other opportunities would she have had to share them with her classmates and peers?

The opportunity these children had to share and explain their culture to teachers and classmates was a source of pride for them. In order to create such opportunities we make every effort to find families that reflect the diversity of each local community to be part of our program. Students, teachers and schools need the energy of family and community. The shorter the distance between the culture of the home and the culture of the school, the easier school life is for children. When parents feel welcome, can participate in the life of the school and can be authentically involved in their children's learning, the outlook for the children in terms of academic and social success is vastly improved. This conviction, which has been borne out by research, was a strong component in the philosophy behind the parenting programs I set up in Toronto schools. [2] The staff in these schools developed a deep level of understanding of the different cultures in the neighbourhood when local families brought their babies and toddlers to the parenting programs and stayed involved with the school as their children started kindergarten. With understanding comes respect, and respect creates the conditions for social inclusion.

Canada is one of the world's most successful pluralistic societies. This is in large part due to the legacy of Pierre Elliott Trudeau, who as prime minister spearheaded changes to Canada's policies relating to immigration, and championed multiculturalism as a Canadian value. These changes aimed to reshape Canada as a cultural mosaic, in which the richness of cultures would not be assimilated into a melting pot but would exist side by side, giving strength to one another and to the country as a whole. Trudeau's policies didn't mean the end of racism: we continue to struggle against it as it manifests itself in subtle and not-so-subtle ways. Nor have we eliminated the difficulties many families experience in trying to "fit in"; this experience of exclusion crosses the entire socio-economic spectrum. We have only recently had the humbling experience of learning that a golf club in one of the toniest city neighbourhoods in Canada had an unwritten policy of excluding Jews from membership. Our courts recently concluded a series of trials that dealt with the murder of Reena Virk, a disadvantaged and marginalized teen, who died for the crime of trying hard to belong. The North American challenge is to resist complacency about what we have achieved and to renew our efforts to ensure that we build a truly inclusive society.

Diversity has many aspects. It goes a long way beyond recognizing the multiplicity of races and nationalities of people who have immigrated to North America from different countries to make it their home. Even among people who share the same cultural heritage, you will find many different lifestyles, economic levels, political beliefs, religious beliefs, parenting styles and family configurations. This kind of diversity also deserves respect. You don't have to be from another country, for example, to belong to a non-mainstream religious group that is unfamiliar to your teacher or is mocked by your peers. A child may come from a family whose religious beliefs mean that he is not allowed to join in the singing of the national anthem or (as is the custom in U.S. schools) repeat the Pledge of Allegiance. This child suffers daily through the conflict between being true to his family's beliefs and his desire to fit in with the other children.

Evolving family structures can also challenge a child's struggle for acceptance. One boy, in a Grade 7 Roots of Empathy class, experienced the separation of his parents during the spring break. While Clayton continued to live with his mother, he maintained a close relationship with his father, who had moved to a new life in the neighbourhood with another man. This was a close-knit but poor community where news travels fast. When Clayton returned to school after the break, he ran a gauntlet of taunting in the schoolyard. Discussion in the Roots of Empathy class that week turned to the subject of teasing and cruelty, and Clayton talked about being upset over the schoolyard behaviour. His classmates, responding to his obvious pain, rallied around him, assuring him, "It's none of their business. We won't let anyone pick on you." As we grow into childhood and encounter issues of fairness, equity and entitlement, we learn what we stand for. As we grow a little older we, like these Grade 7 children, take it further and learn what it is we will stand up for. We often exhort children to be honest, or organize good deeds for them to do. We need to encourage and nurture the heroism in what children, like these Grade 7 students, do spontaneously. They may not have had the sophistication to develop a "social action plan," but they certainly knew they wouldn't allow their friend to be humiliated and hurt. They were able to see how Clayton felt, so that they could break through social stigmas and the conditioning of their environment and stand up in solidarity to take action on his behalf. They took the high road on an issue that many adults wouldn't understand or have the guts to challenge—many wouldn't even be able to put the feelings into words. It is a sensitive teacher who can handle situations like these so that the entire class understands the importance of mutual respect for differences.

Born Excluded: Breaking the Pattern

Ingrained poverty, transmitted from generation to generation, can also create a set of conditions that cry out for understanding. At one time, as an initiative to raise awareness with teachers about issues of social inclusion, I ran "lunch and learn" workshops for teachers that had titles like "A Chocolate Bar for Lunch" and "The Wrong Running Shoes." A key goal of the workshops was to build understanding of the challenges faced by children raised in poverty. If a teacher has little or no experience of communities where the stairwells of the apartment buildings smell of urine and every block has a crack house, she may have difficulty understanding why the children bring lunches made of whatever happened to be in the cupboard, or wear clothes that are inappropriate for the weather or don't do their homework. We need to build empathy for families based on an understanding of their particular circumstances, and on respect for the struggles that many parents face.

In these empathy-focused workshops, I talked about how difficult it is to get your child to school on time when you are a single mother who had your baby when you were fifteen years old, and he's supposed to be in class every morning at 8:45. Some teachers were taken aback. They had never thought about that reality in those terms. It takes some adjusting to put yourself in that mother's shoes, and to understand that she's never learned to plan ahead, that her body is still in that teenage "late to bed, late to rise" biological cycle, and getting her son to school every day— let alone on time!—seems like a huge challenge.

I believe all parents, single or partnered, do the best they can with the hand they've been dealt. But too many have been dealt terrible hands. When I worked with mothers who had their children taken from them because of severe abuse or neglect, I listened as they shared the stories of their own childhood. The stories were harrowing histories of the abuse they themselves had endured as children, stories made all the more chilling by the absence of emotion in the women's voices as they recounted them. Because this harsh response from their parents was all they knew in their own childhoods, many believed that this experience was the norm. They rarely complained about being beaten or injured by their parents; they accepted it as the way things are. Often they even attempted to justify their parents' abuse. "I was a bad kid," a woman told me. "My mother had no choice but to punish me, and when I didn't behave, she had to do it harder."

When these women treat their own children badly, they are only repeating the lessons they learned, lessons that began for them in the earliest weeks and months of their lives. Without intervention and support in changing ingrained patterns, this is what people tend to do, and the cycle goes on. Even with intervention and intensive support, it's very tough to turn around the patterns of a lifetime. Research shows that aggression peaks at the age of three, and that training children out of aggressive behaviour has to begin in the early years; therefore it is vital that we have programs that offer parents and future parents the understanding and skills that can break the cycles of abuse and violence.[3] This is at the heart of my parenting programs and is the mission of Roots of Empathy. When I was developing the parenting program referred to in Appendix A, a key strategy was to offer an environment of "learning in context," an environment where the parents were on familiar ground, in their own community, with their own children. When you give poor or undereducated or teenage mothers an opportunity to talk about how they were parented themselves, asking them, "How were you disciplined? How did it make you feel? What was not okay about it? Were you shouted at? What way did people talk to each other at home?" it can open the door to awareness of negative parenting experiences. This awareness is a necessary step in coming to terms with the harshness of the past and becoming receptive to learning how to parent well.

In the Roots of Empathy program, we are able to create this awareness in children in another way, before they become parents. It is more than just talking about demonstrating parenting, it is being involved with it. The discussions built around the family visits anchor the experience for them, making it more relevant to their own lives, more powerful and longer-lasting.

In Labrador, I met a young Innu girl, Mary, whose fifteenth birthday had just passed. She was in a treatment centre for dual addictions. Mary had photos of two young children on her wall, and when I asked if they were her brother and sister, she said, "No, they're my children." That matter-of-fact sentence conveyed the whole story of her life and the life of her community. This Innu community in Labrador, like many Aboriginal communities, historically suffered an assault on their language, culture and dignity. In far too many cases, instead of a passing on of their rich cultural practices in child-raising, there is an intergenerational transmission of dysfunction and hopelessness. Parenting support is inadequate and community structures are struggling to be effective. The result: suffering, with no apparent end in sight.

Through Roots of Empathy we are offering a way to break these intergenerational patterns, not through instruction but through invitation, not by lecturing but by offering students the freedom to think and behave differently. In my discussions with Aboriginal communities, I have found that the values of our program resonate in many ways, particularly in terms of the respect they show for the importance of the family, the emphasis on children developing in the context of their culture, the focus on teaching children not to judge but to understand, respect for the past and shared responsibility for the future. Our society has been trying to resolve situations by throwing money at the problem. But the kind of programs that are offered slide right over the surface of the real issues. You don't fix that young Innu girl's situation by saying, "Here's how to prepare formula and here are some techniques to help you put your kids to bed." You don't fix Mary's situation in her community just by building some new houses. You need to nurture her, you need to nurture the entire community, offering both hope and opportunity.

Roots of Empathy and Social Inclusion

Jason, one of our first Roots of Empathy babies, was born with two club feet. Jason's mother shared her feelings with the children in the class with honesty and generosity. At one point she talked about her disappointment in learning that her newborn infant had this problem. She'd been expecting a perfect baby. And of course one bright little boy said, "But Jason is a perfect baby." How could anyone possibly think that this energetic little baby, so loved by everyone in the class, was anything less than perfect? Maybe what children like this little boy can give us is a new definition of perfection. The babies in our program respond in ways that intuitively convey the intrinsic worth and dignity of each person. We had a parallel experience, of a classroom baby seeking out and making a favourite of a child whose hands were incompletely formed as a result of a birth defect. This boy, who was no stranger to rejection, found himself the centre of positive attention, given new status through a baby's embrace.

Treating children with respect and setting a place for everyone at the table doesn't mean pretending everyone is the same. Seeing the little baby with club feet as perfect doesn't ignore the fact that he needed three surgeries and may have future challenges as he learns to stand and walk. Inclusion goes beyond tolerance and "putting up with" people; it is about "putting out to" them. It is about teaching and responding to the whole child, not just Lydia-who-needs-a-wheelchair. Labelling children as the "Down syndrome child" or the "immigrant child" is a failure of inclusion. It is defining people by their differences and erecting barriers to recognizing their achievements and contributions.

I previously referred to the Roots of Empathy family whose baby was born with a cleft lip and palate. It is not an exaggeration to say that the children in the Grade 5 class fell in love with that baby. In the program, children are encouraged to ask the parents of the baby about the job of child-raising, focusing on issues that particularly concern them. We prepare children to ask their questions in ways that are sensitive and respectful. One day, the children asked the father how he felt about his baby's upcoming surgery. The father answered with remarkable honesty, telling the children, "I feel like I'm betraying him. I'm going to take him to the hospital, with people he doesn't know, and they're going to hurt him, and I'll have to take away his bottle and his soother, the things that comfort him. And because he doesn't understand language, I can't explain it to him."

The mother's response was different. She said simply, "I miss my family." She and her husband had come to Canada on their own, leaving behind a large family in South America. One of the children spoke up, Travis, a ten-year-old boy who was developmentally delayed. He said to the mother, "We are your family." His words of comfort to the mother were evidence of his sense of inclusion in the classroom. Despite Travis's own challenges, despite the fact that he needed help with academic work, he was confident enough to speak for the entire class. He had become a full member in a community of caring. "We are your family," Travis said. Not "I will be your family" but "We are." Empathy and community were alive and well in that classroom, and the boy's contribution demonstrated sophisticated emotional literacy, even if his traditional literacy skills were delayed.

In the classrooms where the Roots of Empathy baby has a disability, the experience of getting to know these babies through their monthly visits to the class changes the children's perception of disabilities. Children see the connections that link all human beings. They are much more accepting of obvious physical conditions like club feet or cleft palate.

Not all challenges are physical ones. In one of our classes, we had a little boy named Bobby who had severe ADHD (attention deficit hyperactivity disorder). In fact, he was in his regular class for only a couple of hours each day; the rest of the time he was in a special class, where the teacher could work intensively with a few children at a time. The discussion was about exclusion. One of the students mentioned Bobby, saying that she would really feel excluded if, like him, she were taken out of the regular class. So the class talked about ways to help Bobby feel more included. There was no talking behind backs going on here; Bobby was part of the discussion.

Temperament had been the subject of an earlier lesson, and the class thought Bobby must have an intense temperament, since he had strong, sudden reactions to things, spoke loudly without seeming to notice that he was interrupting somebody else and would often "lose it." They decided they could help Bobby feel more included by helping him manage his intensity. Not long after, when Bobby came to the class, he was so agitated he kind of tumbled into the room. One of the other boys noticed. He went over and put his arm around Bobby before he even had his coat off. "Hey, Bobby," he said, "it looks like you're cruising for a bruising today." He was basically saying, "How can I help you not have a bad day?"

Those children had created a safety level, a cushion of comfort in the classroom. The message for everyone was that when they needed help, it would be there. Teachers tell us how the tone of the classroom changes as the children get deeper into the Roots of Empathy program: the level of collaboration and kindness goes way up.

Another facet of family life today is the increasing number of homes where children are raised without a father present. Many children have no concept of a nurturing male figure, cannot imagine a father who feeds his child, plays with her, sings to her and rocks her to sleep. When we look for Roots of Empathy families, we do not assume a single, traditional family structure where there are a mother and a father in the family. We encourage the father to visit with the baby as well. We have fathers and mothers who visit together with the baby and sometimes fathers who visit instead of the mother. These fathers have provided some moving and emotional moments in the classroom.

Picture a tall man in a business suit stretched out beside his daughter on the blanket so that she will feel more comfortable in the strange surroundings of the classroom. Think of a father with the build of a footballer player enchanting his son with "Itsy-Bitsy

Spider" as a class of cool Grade 7s are irresistibly drawn into the song. And the most poignant times are when children quiz the father about how much time he spends with the baby, scarcely able to believe this really happens. Our experience in classroom after classroom tells us that there are many, many children who crave this confirmation of the importance of "Dad" in a baby's life. We value what this offers to the children as a model of male nurturing and a way of parenting that can be theirs when they are adults.

Babies are magical in their ability to bring out the nurturing qualities of boys as well as girls. One instructor with a class of Grade 7 students says she was moved to see the boys' faces light up when the baby came into the classroom at each visit. The caring and protectiveness of these young boys, hidden perhaps by the surface bravado so common in preteens, was brought unabashedly to the surface as they had the opportunity to interact with the baby and watch her get to know them. These experiences go a long way towards reinforcing parenting as an "equal opportunity" vocation that brings rewards to both sexes.

Exposure to the range of diversity I have described here is often the source of transformation in learning. So much of what we accept as "a given" or as "just the way things are" is the result of remaining within the narrow confines of a specific community or set of beliefs. But these are not immutable things. Getting to know people of other races or cultures or religions or socio-economic backgrounds allows us to question our assumptions and to look at our own behaviours from a new perspective. The greater the diversity, the broader the perspective that can be brought forward to help in problem-solving. We see this when students work in groups to discuss the picture of a girl who is sad, thinking of ways to respond to her sadness. The solutions cover the gamut of social circumstances and are invariably about the importance of inclusion. Here are some written examples in the children's own spelling:

This girl might have lost someone. I would tell her: 'even if they are not on the same earth, they are alwase in your hart' (*Grade 4 boy*)

I thing that this little girl is upset because her dad and mom got in to a fight. Then they stoped the fight so the little girl went to her parents and asked them why they were fighting and they said that they were just desticreaning (disagreeing) on some thing. So they decided to have a divorsted. Then her mom told her that her dad is going to live somewhere else. I think that I can help this girl by letting her use my phone to call her dad if she had his phone numbers. Because she really loves and misses him really really a lot. (*Grade 4 girl*)

She might have her knee scraped on the black top. She might have saw her brother and called for help but he didn't answer so she feels very sad and hurt. I could taker her back home or if I am near my house I could bring her over and help her out and explain about her brother. (*Grade 5 girl*)

She could be sad because she had a fight with a friend. She feels bad about it but the friend won't talk to her. I could talk to the sad person and the person who she's in the fight with. I could see what might be the problem and try and help. (*Grade 5 girl*)

Maybe because someone was racist because of her skin colour (the drawing was coloured dark in pencil). Maybe I'd tell them that everyon's skin colour is out of dust and tell them that it's not the outside that counts, it's the inside that counts. (*Grade 6 boy*)

Her mother or father might have cancer. I would let her know I feel sorry. (*Grade 6 boy*)

Maybe people were making fun of the way she looks and tease her and call her names. I would go up to her and sit beside her and ask her if she'd like to hang out with me and my friends. Then I would sit with her and talk. (*Grade 6 girl*)

Every person we meet can teach us something about what it means to be human and what we have to gain when our world values inclusion.

Ins and Outs

Inclusion at school works to ensure that children of all races and children with disabilities have an equal and respected place in the classroom. An inclusionary society would go beyond this, to challenge all the grounds on which a person can be made to feel inferior or shunned or excluded. We see in our schools, more acutely than ever before, another, pervasive kind of exclusion based on whether a child has the right kind of sneakers or is good at the right kinds of sports or lives in the right part of the school district. The social dynamics in schools today are all about innies and outies, and we're not talking about belly-buttons.

Come with me to any school, in a small town or in a big city, and watch the children as they pour through the doors after the recess bell. See the group of little girls over there, already unwinding their skipping ropes and starting a game of double dutch. And here's a group of boys playing tag near the trees. They are engaged in the natural exuberance of the playground. But do you see that little boy, almost hidden behind the tree, his face wistful as he watches the others play? Or the girl leaning with her back against the wall, casting occasional glances towards her classmates as they laugh and skip rope? They are experiencing the pain of exclusion. They may, on the surface and through our adult eyes, look just like their classmates. There are no obvious differences in skin colour or ability setting them apart. Yet they are marginalized and their pain is very real.

Not all children are blessed with friendship. When teams are chosen, or when friends gather around a table at lunch, pick seats on the school bus, pass out birthday invitations or exchange Valentine cards, certain children are repeatedly, consistently left out. This does not have to be accompanied by overt bullying or name-calling for the child to feel the pain of being excluded. As humans we ache to belong, to be someone's friend, to be invited in. As children we feel it particularly keenly, so much so in fact that being left out can be disabling; it can cast a shadow over our openness to learning and can interfere with our social and emotional development.

Roots of Empathy tackles this head-on. The discussions we have in class about emotions include engaging children in responding to scenarios that deal with social inclusion. In small groups the children will explore issues such as embarrassment or bullying, and discuss the feelings these situations evoke and ways to solve the problems they create. Every child knows what "fair" means; they know what it feels like when they themselves are treated unfairly, and in the scenario discussions, they take the perspective of others, exploring what it must feel like to them. The next step is: What do you do about it? Do you *stand by* or do you *stand up for it*? Roots of Empathy teaches children to challenge injustice wherever they see it. The scenario group work includes coming up with specific actions to take to intervene in an unfair situation. The building of empathy sets the stage for caring, altruistic action.

Most of us have still-vivid memories of being excluded when we were children, and guilty recollections of the times we joined in and were equally unkind to other children. Because it is so prevalent, we have come to believe that it is part of human nature. Some people will comment that "kids have always been cruel to each other, there's nothing you can do about it." That's not good enough. In Roots of Empathy, children are taught that they are condoning injustice, unkindness and cruelty if they witness it and do nothing. Children learn to follow routines at school, they learn not to use physical force to solve disagreements. If we help them they can learn to treat each other with kindness and respect. In this way, actively every classroom can become a force for peace and cooperation.

While children of vastly different backgrounds sometimes do find a common bond, they are the exception. More often than not, in selecting their friends, children will gravitate towards other's who are similar to them. That's what they base their connection on. Rich kids want to be with other rich kids, the athletic kids with other kids who like sports, and so on. Like hunter-gatherers of old, they are still seeking out those tribes where they know they belong, and know what's expected of them. Some children readily find their group and settle in. They are the fortunate ones, but even they often worry that in next year's class, or two years down the road, they won't find their niche so easily. At various stages of childhood, friendships shift and develop around different things: proximity, common hobbies, kindred spirits. But in every school, in every class, you will always find a handful of excluded children, and their lives are hell. A seven-year-old girl who is a victim of bullying got a tummy ache every Sunday night at the thought of having to face another week of being frightened and humiliated at school. Keely in Grade 8 wrote of her pain: "My two friends, who walked to school with me every single day, decided to walk over my front lawn and not pick me up. They pretended they didn't know me. I felt sick in my stomach because my friends didn't include me." Children like Keely are truly suffering. That suffering has got to stop.

In one of our Grade 7 classes, the teacher asked the students about feeling left out. Someone mentioned picking teams in the gym and how painful it is when you are the last one chosen and you don't know why, and someone else mentioned feeling left out in conversations when you don't know what the other people are talking about. Several Muslim girls said they felt left out because their family traditions didn't allow them to join any of the after-school clubs. Ivan, who was brand new to Canada and to the class, said he felt left out because he didn't have any friends. At first there was silence. Then a boy at Ivan's table said, "I'm your friend." There were a few more moments of silence. A voice from the back of the room said, "I'm your friend." There was a ping-pong effect as every single student in the room quietly repeated one after the other "I am your friend."

Most children experiencing this isolation suffer in silence. They will swallow their pain and hide their loneliness and sense of misery, even from their families. Others will act out in school, sometimes disrupting the class or getting into playground squabbles, unwittingly adding to their experience of exclusion. In the Grade 7 class just described, an environment of safety and trust had been established. The children felt comfortable enough to speak up and their classmates rose to the occasion, offering friendship and help. The work they had done together allowed them to translate empathy into action, to experience a sense of solidarity and true altruism.

Too many children are unable to learn because they are in so much social pain. The job description for teachers is an ever-expanding one as they meet the challenge of ensuring that the conditions for learning are in place. The child who is in emotional pain from feeling excluded does not have the heart for learning. What happens to the child on the playground at lunchtime can have a tremendous effect on the child's education. Being ready and able to learn is more than having enough sharpened pencils and paper; the child needs to be emotionally ready as well. That can't happen when the child feels like an outcast in the classroom.

Teachers have a uniquely rich opportunity to help children see through the lens of equity and social compassion. We can encourage children to think about what is fair, right and just, and to have empathy for others. The ideas that we introduce through Roots of Empathy are often built on by the classroom teacher who knows the children well and has access to more "teachable moments." In the society of the classroom, exclusion often turns on issues much smaller than race or religion. It may be about status, money, looks, intelligence or athletic ability. But the principle of bridging those differences is the same.

It is a measure of a school's commitment to inclusion when they place a premium on celebrating citizenship. I don't mean citizenship certificates that are a consolation prize for the kids who didn't win in sports or come top of the class in science. I mean real recognition of acts of kindness, support for others, caring and friendship. Do we value kindness as much as we value scoring goals in a hockey game? Do we value compassion and helpfulness as much as getting an A in math?

Building Inclusion

Building an inclusive classroom or community goes beyond breaking down the barriers that create exclusion. There has to be positive, purposeful acts of inclusion.

The desired result of these acts is to honour our interconnectedness and celebrate the strength that comes from interdependence. Making room for those who have been excluded, with all their needs and aspirations, takes nothing away from those who are not ready. The reverse is true. Along with needs and inherent in aspirations are enormously rich contributions that raise the quality of experience for everyone. An inclusive, interdependent society combines judgment with empathy for those who suffer most. We are all enriched.

With little or no encouragement, children want this kind of world. The baby on the green Roots of Empathy blanket who is trying hard but unsuccessfully to reach a toy, just has to catch the eye of one of the children in the circle. The need is understood. Help is spontaneously, unquestioningly given. Our job as adults, parents and teachers is to foster an environment where each of us—including the smallest and least advantaged— can rely on pervasive and constant cooperation, acceptance and respect.

SECTION THREE

Roots of Empathy and Society

This final section takes the wisdom we have learned from our Roots of Empathy babies and illustrates how that wisdom can spread beyond the classroom and give support to critical aspects of the movement to build caring, peaceful and civil societies.

We have explored the meaning of empathy and its vital role in the development of strong human connection and healthy social institutions. We have connected the strands that offer children a tapestry of social and emotional competence. We have seen how a baby represents a pure force for unlocking in us the capacity for authentic, empathic relationships.

The final chapters explore how the lessons of Roots of Empathy, and the philosophy at its core, affect how we challenge injustice, how we live and care for each other, and how we take responsibility for the safekeeping of our planet.

WHAT BABIES WOULD SAY TO BULLIES

Seven-year-old Timothy holds up his picture and explains what he has drawn. "This is my friend, and he is sad."

"Why is he sad?" I ask.

"Because this other boy spit on him."

"And what did you do?"

"I wiped off the spit and I told the other boy not to do it anymore."

THE SCHOOLYARD BULLYING SCENE in which one child spits at another child is played out daily in playgrounds around the world. What usually does not happen is that a child of seven comes to the aid of the victim. Not only does he support the victim, wiping the spit off his face, but he teaches the perpetrator that it is not okay to spit at others. Timothy has taken on the role of peacemaker and has raised the bar of civility in the playground, translating empathy into action, an approach we could wish for from world governments.

I am encouraged to think about Timothy and the millions of other children who take these small steps to ease the sadness of their friends and to end the rule of the bully. This child demonstrated clearly and simply what is needed: someone to comfort and befriend the victim and to stand up to the bully.

In a society where parents and teachers are increasingly worried about the damaging effects of bullying, Roots of Empathy is recognized as a program that offers solutions. Our program approaches bullying in a unique fashion. Rather than targeting the bully or victim, Roots of Empathy sees the classroom as a unit of change, a small community, and teaches messages of social justice that reach onlookers, bullies and victims alike. The picture emerging from research on the program shows that it is working.

I recently accompanied Dr. Al Ainsley-Green, the newly appointed Children's Commissioner for England, on a visit to a Grade 2 Roots of Empathy classroom in Manitoba, Canada. The children asked him questions at the end of the visit such as "How did you get here?" "Have you met the Queen?" "Does England have sharks?" and poignantly "Do you have war in England?" After respectful responses to the children's questions the Commissioner asked the children to tell him about bullying. William's hands shot up and in a clear, sure voice he said, "I used to be a bully—I used to bully Samantha and Mark and Aiden." "And me," said Garth, "he used to bully me." William nodded. "That's right I used to bully Garth too, but I'm not a bully anymore." William qualified that he learned self-control and how not to bully from Roots of Empathy.

Research into the efficacy of the program was begun in 2000 by the University of British Columbia under the leadership of

Dr. Clyde Hertzman. The principal investigator, Dr. Kimberly Schonert-Reichl, in reporting results from the first two years, confirmed marked changes in children who had participated in the program. These children demonstrated more advanced emotional understanding and pro-social behaviour. On measures of aggression, the children in the Roots of Empathy classes showed significant reduction both in "proactive" aggression, a kind of aggression synonymous with overt bullying, and in "relational or social aggression," which is associated with "back-stabbing" and other exclusionary behaviour, and could be described as covert bullying. (The research is described more fully in Appendix B to this book, see page 239)

The very encouraging story told by the research is reinforced for me daily by the art and writing of children in classrooms across the country, and by anecdotes sent to me by parents, teachers and Roots of Empathy instructors. In one classroom, when the instructor was encouraging children to talk about a time when they were bullied or someone they knew was bullied, nine-year-old Sam said, "Is it okay to talk about it if you were the bully?" What ensued reminded me of a child's version of the South African Truth and Reconciliation led by Bishop Desmond Tutu. Sam told the class that he'd been threatening a kid in Grade 1 and taking his lunch money from him. The response from the class? "That's a very hard thing to own up to." Sam was commended by his classmates for his courage in confessing to his bullying behaviour and the discussion moved on to what he needed to do to make amends. It was agreed that Sam should apologize to the Grade 1 student and give him back the money he took. When it emerged that the now "ex-bully" didn't have enough money, the rest of the children chipped in pennies and dimes to make up the amount. Intent on collaborating on doing the right thing, these children ensured that self-respect and social justice triumphed over humiliation, shame and damaging isolation.

Lack of hope is an epidemic; children who are bullied are often devoid of hope, that frail connection to the future, and in the most dramatic of cases hopelessness can lead to suicide in children. The youngest known victim in the United Kingdom was only eight years old.[1] The toll among Canadian adolescents, such as Dawn Marie Wesley[2] and Emmet Fralik[3], hounded and bullied by their peers, is frighteningly high and on the rise. There is no keener revelation of the soul of a society than the attention it pays to its vulnerable. Children who are victims of bullying are vulnerable and should not be expected to heal themselves. Skilled adult intervention is required, but more importantly, preventative interventions, like Roots of Empathy, are essential.

The World of Bullying

Bullying is fundamentally an act of cruelty. It involves the repeated abuse of social power. It is a form of violence. Bullying doesn't always look the same, and adults need to learn to recognize it in all its manifestations. The stereotypical bully is the bigger kid who physically attacks someone smaller, perhaps with the help and support of his friends. But bullying doesn't have to involve a physical attack. The threat of violence can be equally intimidating and sometimes more terrifying to the child who is constantly vigilant and on edge, waiting for the attack. Children's lives can also be made unbearable by a constant stream of insults and hurtful comments or by fear of having their property stolen or damaged or by being excluded.

A cowardly form of bullying unheard of a few years ago, but which is now dramatically on the increase, is "cyberbullying." Through the faceless medium of e-mail, chat rooms, and cell phone text messaging, bullies can stealthily target their victims, terrorizing them with threats and exposing them to ridicule and humiliation. While it may be difficult enough for adults to discover and intervene in face-to face bullying, it is virtually impossible to detect the cyberbully until the damage is done, the victim is targeted and scores of "cyber-bystanders" are implicated.

Not all bullies are boys; girl bullies do exist. The previously mentioned case of Reena Virk is a tragic example, and although it is comparatively rare for girls to use physical violence as a means of intimidating others, it is not unheard of. It is still a fact of life in our society that girls are socialized, significantly more than boys, to place importance on relationships and to master their social world through interpersonal exchanges and negotiation. The socialization process for girls also makes engaging in physical aggression unappealing for girls because it is considered to be "unfeminine." Little wonder then that when situations turn negative, the weapons of choice will be relationship-based and the damage inflicted will be emotional and very personal.

Studies on bullying show that girls are more likely to bully through social aggression. Marion K. Underwood in her comprehensive investigation in *Social Aggression Among Girls*, notes, "Girls hurt each other's feelings by social exclusion via sneers, verbal comments, nasty notes, gossip and electronic mail. Girls hurt each other's friendships by spreading ugly rumours about those they do not like and by manipulating those they do like by saying 'I won't be your friend if you don't . . . (do what I say).'"

Through social aggression, the bully can isolate or exclude a classmate, making her feel alone in the middle of a busy classroom. The bully may spread malicious gossip or create an organized campaign to drive away another girl's friends.[4] While such bullying is commonly directed at the weak and unpopular, this is not always the case, and we, as adults, need to be vigilant and aware that things are not always as they seem.

I know of one case where the victim was academically successful, a strong athlete, musical and beautiful. Yet she was vilified by her classmates, ostracized because of her gifts and refused friendship as a strategy for bringing her down a peg or two. These bullying tactics may not leave physical scars or injuries, but they are just as emotionally devastating to the victim. The lack of overt violence should not deceive us into underestimating the impact of this kind of bullying; we ignore it at our peril.

The Impact of Bullying

The prevalence and increasingly violent manifestations of bullying point to the urgency of putting in place solutions that are known to work. Most studies show that bullying directly involves at least 15 per cent of schoolchildren.[5] That means that in any given school with a student population of five hundred, seventy-five children are either bullying or being bullied. How many more are affected because they are drawn, however reluctantly, into a circle of support for the bully? And how many are left in a state of anxiety or shame because they are witnesses to the bullying and feel powerless to intervene? When you add it all up, you have the potential to turn an environment where every child should feel safe into a threatening, hostile landscape. And it doesn't end there.

The effects are long-lasting for all concerned. Children who display aggressive, antisocial behaviours at an early age are more likely to become delinquents in their teens and in adult life. Studies by Dr. Richard Tremblay, a renowned researcher and an authority on childhood aggression, point to physical aggression in the early years as a key predictor of involvement in crime at a later age.[6] A study by Professor Dan Olweus, recognized internationally as an expert on bullying, found that by age twenty-four, 60 per cent of individuals who had been identified in Grades 6 to 9 as aggressive children have at least one criminal conviction. By adulthood, identified bullies had more court convictions, alcoholism and antisocial personality disorders, and used more mental-health services than the others in the study.[7]

The victims of bullying carry the scars into their adult lives. They become more anxious and insecure and experience lower self-esteem. The psychological damage they suffer affects their emotional, social and academic development and has far-reaching consequences. Although adulthood provides the victims with greater choice over the environment in which they live and work, they still are more likely to suffer from depression and lack of self-confidence than individuals who have not been the victims of bullying.

Even the children who never become victims are harmed when they see bullying taking place and nothing being done about it. They can be paralyzed by their sense of powerlessness to intervene, or they may live in fear of being victimized themselves. Seeing no negative consequences for the bully, they may even decide that aggression is a valid approach to resolving conflict or getting one's way.

Bullies Are Made and Can Be Unmade

Where do bullies come from? It is a common characteristic of bullies that they have an impulsive temperament and are easily provoked to aggressive or violent behaviour. Family environment is a strong influence in the development of aggressive behaviours. Aggression is a trait we are born with. It peaks around age three and, for most people, drops steadily after that age. Learning to regulate aggression starts with what we experience in the home. Dr. Richard Tremblay has reported on family patterns that strongly relate to aggression.[8] If conflicts in the home are solved by the use of force or by controlling or bullying behaviour, this is the model the child will learn to use in his own relationships with others. When this is coupled with a lack of warm, nurturing care and inattention to the child's needs, the child is left without resources to develop pro-social behaviour towards others. They have no sense of empathy for their victims and little or no remorse about their bullying activities. There is widespread agreement that bullies have not developed the skills to understand the perspective of others and consequently lack empathy.

Most of us can recall egregious bullying incidents from our own childhoods, incidents in which we saw one child relentlessly tormented by another or by a group. Perhaps we were one of those children, either the tormented or the tormentors. Too often in the past those incidents were ignored by teachers and other adults or dismissed as the natural rough-and-tumble of the schoolyard. And not enough has changed, even today. When adults appear to be condoning aggressive acts, or at least turning a blind eye to them, it serves to support the bullying behaviour, since children are quick to pick up on the unspoken messages the adults are giving. In such circumstances, most children who are bullied either do not report it to adults or wait a very long time before doing so. They are embarrassed and afraid of retaliation from the bully, and their expectations of helpful responses from the adults are usually low.

Research has conclusively shown that the once-popular hands-off approach isn't helpful. Bullying is not a rite of passage; it is not a necessary part of growing up. It is critical that adults send a clear message that bullying behaviour is wrong and has to stop. When bullying is not challenged, it is allowed to fester. The victims continue to suffer and their future is compromised as they often become depressed or withdraw from social interaction, missing countless days of school in their attempts to avoid the harassment of the schoolyard.

The way we deal with bullying is a measure of what we value. In the discussion of emotional literacy in chapter 8, I talked about the "zero tolerance" policies in schools. After a number of highly publicized and extreme incidents of violence in schools, many school districts and jurisdictions have introduced these policies which impose automatic penalties for a range of infractions, including violent behaviour in school. They allow less scope for teachers and school administrators to exercise judgment around either the circumstances of the incident itself or the personal circumstances of the student involved. In incidents of bullying, that may mean the bully—and sometimes even the victim—is suspended, given detentions, or otherwise isolated. This may create the perception of direct action being taken, but it is ineffective in bringing about any lasting change. During his week away from school or his hours in the detention room, does the bully learn anything about why bullying is wrong and how he can more effectively relate to his classmates? Is the victim counselled to respond to others in a way that doesn't invite bullying? Will the class as a whole have an opportunity to contribute to solutions to the bullying problem? The toxic effects of bullying will not be solved by punitive measures and isolation, or, even worse, by placing the bully in a holding tank with other offenders and no alternative role models.

Roots of Empathy Tackles Bullying

How, then, can we tackle bullying in an effective way, within both our schools and our communities? Bully patrols and surveillance cameras in the schoolyard may become necessary to respond to bullying once it is entrenched, but Roots of Empathy is about prevention; it is about bully-proofing from the inside out. The development of social and emotional competence and empathy throughout the program awakens the sense of moral responsibility in children so that they become their own police. When the motivation for justice is a part of our internal moral landscape, we are not dependent on authoritarian structures to transform our behaviour; we have internalized the principles that allow us to respond in a socially responsible way. If we help children learn to challenge cruelty, they gain a sense of their own efficacy in confronting injustice. We build children's emotional literacy by

- showing them a pure example of emotions in their baby
- creating a safe environment in the classroom so that they have a secure platform for discussing their feelings
- helping them learn to regulate those feelings.

The children have the tools in the language of emotional literacy and the empathy that grows from this, to take social action against injustice, not in the form of fists and nasty words but in the form of standing up against what they call "meanness" and things being "unfair."

In our classrooms, bullying is presented as one of many ways that people can experience emotional pain. Children are both taught to be and naturally become advocates for their Roots of Empathy baby. They create solidarity in the classroom when, in relation to the baby, they can all agree on what they care about and a standard of social behaviour. When the instructor asks the children, "How would you feel if your Roots of Empathy baby was bullied or excluded?" there is a consensus of righteous indignation. Our program advocates for and discusses the notion that every child has a right to justice, a right to a level playing field at school, and a right not to be mocked, bullied or excluded because of immutable factors like race, ethnicity or physical appearance. This principle works against the kind of environment that allowed a group of teenagers in Victoria, B.C., to use the power of the clique to mock, abuse and, ultimately, cause the death of Reena Virk, a child who was different from them and sought desperately and vainly to belong. Children in Roots of Empathy learn how to be good citizens in the community of their classroom. They realize that by inaction in cases of witnessed injustice, such as bullying, we condone the injustice by not speaking out against it.

In the classroom, we create an atmosphere of safety and acceptance for every child. We talk about emotions in a way that shows
we value and accept them. The classroom teacher and Roots of
Empathy instructor will share their own feelings and their memories of difficult, sad or scary experiences from their childhood.
This encourages the children to feel that they can tell the teacher if
they are experiencing or witnessing bullying. A discussion of bullying in one class led to the teacher sharing a vivid memory of her
own childhood. Her mother had hand-tailored a coat for her, and
she became the target of children in the schoolyard who taunted
her because she wasn't wearing a store-bought coat. They pushed
her to the ground and, straddling her, they drew a line with white
chalk down the centre of her back. While she was telling her story,
she was surprised to find herself tearful as the pain resurfaced and
caught her by surprise. Her emotion was reflected on the faces
of the children sitting in the circle around her.

This understanding of others and the ability to see things from
another person's perspective provides the foundation for the
development of strong pro-social skills. These are the skills that
most victims and bullies seem to lack.

We advocate a sense of community where we have civic concern for each other and no one is a bystander. We all have a responsibility to reach out and intervene—or seek out help to achieve
that intervention if necessary—when we see something that
is wrong.

In one of our Roots of Empathy exercises we ask the primary
grade children to draw a picture of a time they helped someone
who was sad. This exercise helps the children to identify emotions
and to value their own ability to help others. It also gives them
the message that, when we encounter someone who is unhappy,
or when one of our friends is sad or distressed, we are expected to
help. It gives children a sense of power; they may not be able to
solve all the problems of the world, but they can make a difference

to one person. They can help. When the students share their responses to this, it is inspiring to the whole class. They see the many ways that children just like them have helped their classmates, their siblings, even the adults in their lives.

Using the power of storytelling is a strong component of the program. Literature is a person's perspective of a piece of the world in time and space; it opens doors to feelings and provides a common experience for all children. The instructor uses storybooks to explore and open discussion on a range of themes, building bridges between the emotions explored in the story and the children's own experiences. These books are specially chosen to complement the curriculum and to stimulate discussion appropriate to the age group of the children. The books related to bullying make it easier for children, who might be embarrassed or worried to talk about their own experiences, to explore the perspective of the character in the story. The exploration opens insights for the child that can validate feelings and shape solutions. The range of bullying scenarios that children write about offers poignant insights into the experiences that hurt and frighten them:

> I once got bullied by two other kids in kindergarten. Everyday, the two girls put rocks on the slide and they were the only ones allowed to go down the slide. They threw rocks at me. (*Kindergarten*)

> Somebody was saying to me, "give me your money or I will chase you," and that means he is going to beat me up. It's not good to bully someone. (*Grade 1*)

> My friend was being bullied by being called mean names because of her skin colour. I was scared, but I said, "don't say mean names." They hurt my friend's feelings. (*Grade 2*)

Someone bullied me the other day at recess. He grabbed me by the shirt. I didn't cry until later. (*Grade 3*)

I went to the bathroom during lunchtime, and when I tried to leave, two girls wouldn't let me. When I cried, and begged them to let me out of the bathroom, they said I was a crybaby. When the teacher came, they said I made it up. (*Grade 5*)

When I was walking in the hall, two boys came behind me and started pulling my bra strap. They laughed at me and said, "Let's see your hooters." I felt very embarrassed. (*Grade 7*)

Children then work in groups to examine these bullying scenarios and develop responses that will not only help the victim but send out the clear message that bullying is not acceptable.

Bringing Roots of Empathy into a school is a conscious decision to create an environment where bullying cannot flourish. The teachers involved in the program are part of a whole school community where each person has a role in stopping and preventing bullying behaviours. The principles of respect, inclusion and empathy that are basic to the program are also the foundation to building a classroom where bullying is not tolerated and where children can feel part of a safe community. Roots of Empathy teachers understand the impact of intervening when bullying happens, not only for the bully and the victim, but for the powerful example it provides to the children witnessing this behaviour. The child who learns the skills to intervene feels good inside when the opportunity to challenge cruelty presents itself. When schools are committed to creating an environment free of bullying, the results go beyond protecting victims. The entire school population sees an improvement in the level of learning, in children feeling safe and self-confident at school and in the development of more positive relationships.

An instructor told me that one day her Roots of Empathy class was scheduled right after recess. This was not a family-visit day, but a post-visit session—and bullying was the planned topic of discussion. Even before she could bring up the topic, Paulo told her and the rest of the class that he had been bullied on the playground. Other kids had called him an idiot and pushed him around. The other students told Paulo how sorry they were that this happened, talked about how they would feel if it happened to them and offered a number of actions they could take if they were bullied or saw someone else being bullied. Paulo, relieved that he had worked up the courage to tell his classmates what had happened to him, felt included in a supportive circle and told the instructor that the class had "made him feel a whole lot better."

Every Child a Force for Peace

Roots of Empathy is not an overnight cure for bullying. It's not a short-term intervention tactic aimed at those who bully. Its approach is broad, deep and preventative. It builds a culture that values inclusion, responds in caring and practical ways to the victims, and nurtures in all children a respect for and sense of responsibility to one another.

We respect the prerequisites for peace when we feel imagination, faith and hope in the classroom. In the words of Gandhi, "If we want to have peace in the world, we have to start with the children." In our program we believe in the power of children to shape the future, so that there can be civic participation and equity of access for all. It is differences that form the basis of bullying, whether a child has the "wrong" body shape, accent, parents, friends, or clothes, or comes from the "wrong" part of town. In Roots of Empathy we eclipse these obvious differences, pulling a thread of connection between the sameness we unfold as we speak of our feelings. The thin varnish that covers our egos disappears as children discover the comfort of connection. Differences are acknowledged, our principle of inclusion embraces the mutable and immutable, but our true celebration is grounded in the commonalities of humanity and in our feeling, empathic selves.

12

WHAT BABIES
WOULD SAY ABOUT
INFANT SAFETY

neur siak
o Bear.

A s children in the Roots of Empathy program follow the development of their baby in the first year of life, the opportunities to focus on many aspects of infant safety occur naturally. With every milestone the baby reaches, her range of skills increases and so does the range of things that can be a threat to her safety. As each milestone is reached, students are encouraged to think about and discuss what dangers might now exist in the baby's environment that her parents have to protect her from.

Crying and Safety

In her first months, before she is independently mobile, one of her significant skills and essential methods of communication is crying. As mentioned earlier, in my years in the parenting field I have often worked with teen mothers who believed that babies shouldn't cry, and that responding to a crying baby would spoil the baby. On one occasion I saw a baby just learning to walk, who fell hard and hurt himself. When the baby started to cry, the mother commented, "No pain, no gain." Not only would she not pick up the baby herself, she refused to let me pick him up, and told the baby, "You're so bad. Stop that crying." Some parents will apply this "tough love" approach to very young children in the mistaken belief that it will help them cope better with the harshness of life later on. The opposite is true. Early nurturing and responsive care enhance a child's resilience and ability to cope with adversity. The values and patterns of parenting are transmitted from one generation to the next, and if these are negative values and destructive patterns, it is the responsibility of a caring society to give a new generation an alternative model.

When a baby's distress is responded to with impatience or not responded to at all, crying can be one of the most dangerous things a baby can do. Parents who believe that a crying baby is being bad, is trying to manipulate them or is a wimp are likely to become angry at the baby who cries persistently, and sometimes that anger results in violence against the baby, such as shaking, throwing or hitting. All children in Roots of Empathy classrooms learn about Shaken Baby Syndrome, which can cause serious brain damage and even death.

The approach to sharing information about this kind of danger to babies is sensitively tailored to the age group of the students. Consequently the children are not frightened by the information;

they use it to become strong advocates for the prevention of harm to babies. Children don't need protection from the truth, but they do need a supportive adult to help them make sense of events that can be frightening. An eight-year-old boy from one of our classes, when visiting a pregnant cousin, earnestly cautioned the mother-to-be: "If your baby cries a lot, you can't ever, ever shake it. No matter how frustrated you get or how loud it cries, you have to put the baby in the crib, leave the room, and then you can call a friend or have a hot drink." A child advocate of the first order, this little boy is carrying significant public-health messages in a meaningful way.

The message of preventing harm to babies is one that the children take to heart. When we ask them to write about this lesson afterwards they tell us, "You should never shake a baby. It could hurt the baby's brain and if you can't stop the baby crying, put it in the crib and close the door and call someone to help you."

In our program, we emphasize the uniqueness of each human being and the importance of not labelling a baby as good or bad. We actively teach the children that a baby who is crying is not a "bad" baby but a baby with a problem, and the adults need to help solve the problem. That's being responsive. To help children understand this concept, the instructor will wonder out loud about the baby. The baby cries, and the instructor engages the children in a problem-solving exercise. "I wonder if he's crying because he's hungry? Let's ask his mommy if he needs to be breastfed. I wonder if he's crying because he's tired of lying on his back? Let's try helping him roll over. I wonder if he's crying because his head is heavy, and he's frustrated because he can't hold his head up for long when he lies on his tummy, and he wants to look at us?"

Taking their cue from the instructor, the children try to figure out what is happening by taking the physical perspective of the baby. Very soon they can identify a long list of possible reasons why the baby might be fussing or crying. The next step is to develop a parallel list of strategies to try to help solve the baby's problem. Since the first year of life is the most critical in terms of accidental injuries and maltreatment, it is yet another reason that the Roots of Empathy program focuses on babies.

The children in our classes impress me with the empathy they feel for the parents and caregivers who shake their babies out of ignorance and frustration. Many, like the little boy above, seem to take on a personal mission of warning new parents they meet about the hazards of shaking a baby, and of responding appropriately to crying. The first year that Roots of Empathy was offered in Manitoba, the local media ran a story about a baby who had died after being shaken by his father. The students in the program started to talk about it with their homeroom teacher during a current affairs discussion. The teacher, who had been extending Roots of Empathy learning into regular classes, had been concerned about what the students' reactions would be to the media story. Would they be ready with the "should haves" and "could haves"? Would they vent their anger at this father whose child had just died? Although very upset and sad that a child had died, the students' first reaction was "Can you imagine how bad this dad must feel?" "How scared and alone he must feel in jail? If only he had known what to do." "If only he had put the baby in a safe place until he was calm." The feelings expressed by the students demonstrated an all-encompassing level of empathy that included sadness at a preventable infant death and insights into the horror the parent would feel in the aftermath of an explosive moment. When the classroom teacher later shared this discussion with her colleagues in the staff room, they were stunned—not only by the mature, compassionate response of the students but by their handling of the complexity of moral issues involved.

Sleep and Safety: Are You Ready to Be a Parent?

Sleep looms large in the lives of babies and young children—and in the lives of their parents. In our program, studying sleep offers the opportunity to focus on the importance of routine in the life of a baby and young child. Routines help children predict and understand what's coming next and make transitions easier. When we talk about the fact that little babies wake up several times during the night, the children recognize how hard it is for new parents to struggle out of sleep to attend to the baby's needs. Through talking with the baby's parent in class, children come to understand that caring for a baby is a twenty-four-hour-a-day job. Students in Grades 7 and 8 are particularly attuned to the issue of sleep deprivation. They listen acutely as the Roots of Empathy parents talk of feeling constantly tired, irritable, sluggish, indecisive and sometimes depressed. Frequently, these students say they couldn't handle being wakened so much and would not want to have children until they are "way, way older." The huge demands of parenthood are brought vividly home to the senior students, and they have no trouble connecting it to the enormous restrictions teen pregnancy would bring to their lives. More than this, the baby in the classroom is a person, not a concept. Their relationship with the Roots of Empathy family gives them a sense of the responsibility for another human being that one takes on in becoming a parent. They come to understand how their inexperience could jeopardize a real person's life and that it goes far beyond cutting short their own responsibility-free youth and their own dreams.

When we discuss infant safety in relation to sleep, the issue of sudden infant death syndrome (SIDS) is addressed. As with our discussion of Shaken Baby Syndrome, the way information is shared respects the developmental stage of the children and care is taken to ensure that it does not invoke fear. SIDS, the sudden unexpected death of an otherwise healthy baby under one year of age, occurs while the baby is sleeping, and often leaves parents stunned and disabled by guilt. Parents of babies who die unexpectedly like this go through long periods of "what if's" and "if only's," blaming themselves. SIDS is still considered a mystery and is largely unpreventable.

The one preventative measure that has been shown to be effective in reducing the incidence of SIDS by as much as 50 per cent, although the reasons for this are not fully understood, is the practice of putting the baby to sleep on his or her back. It is this aspect of SIDS that we focus on in the classroom. Every child in a Roots of Empathy classroom learns the public-health message: *Put babies to sleep on their backs.* From feedback, we know that the children are sharing the information with their families and family friends who have babies. At the end of the year, when students write evaluations and reflections of what they have learned, a majority of them highlight SIDS and Shaken Baby Syndrome as important new knowledge they have acquired.

Mobile Baby, Safe Home

As students interact with their baby over the school year, the baby is steadily growing from an infant quietly snuggled in her parent's arms, to an energetic, sitting, rolling, grasping, crawling, standing, walking dynamo. As each of these milestones is reached, the students consider the dangers and safety threats to which the baby is now exposed. For example, being able to grasp things means that the baby can pick up all kinds of dangerous items, like coins, buttons or Lego pieces, and put them in her mouth. The children talk about how the baby doesn't yet understand that these things can choke her and it is up to the adults to keep them out of her reach. These discussions teach children to predict and think ahead to consequences, a lesson that is also applied to their own experiences.

The fact that a crawling baby can move quickly and head directly to electrical cords and outlets or to the top of a flight of stairs—yet another set of dangers—reinforces for children the lesson that a baby must never be left unsupervised and that parents have a huge responsibility to be vigilant always. Depending on the age level of students, these lessons in infant safety are further anchored through group work on safeproofing or through artwork that allows students to express what is dangerous for a baby. We are growing citizens who will advocate and plan for public safety. Making "doorknob safety signs" is an activity children tackle with enthusiasm. Instead of a Do Not Disturb sign hanging from a bedroom doorknob, imagine a picture of a pair of big eyes looking down on a baby crawling into a turned-over trashcan and a message that warns, "Keep your eyeballs on Me!!"

No Safe Amount: Alcohol and Tobacco

When we talk with students about the growth of the baby's brain and body, we offer information about the incredible changes a baby goes through, not only in his first year of life but in the nine months before he was born. As well as all the positive things that help a baby to grow, such as good nutrition, stimulation and, most of all, love, we ensure that students are made aware of the things that imperil that optimal growth.

Children, who hate the smell of cigarettes, can easily appreciate that exposing people, especially babies, to second-hand smoke is bad for their health. We primarily focus on negative outcomes such as low birth weight if a mother smokes while pregnant. A tiny, underweight baby will have lungs that don't work as well as those of a normal-weight baby and will have many other struggles that could have been prevented if his parents had had a smoke-free home. Children are deservedly acknowledged as the powerful advocates behind our successful anti-smoking campaigns.

The urgency of convincing children of this health message is increasing as new findings emerge on the causes of aggression. While there is no single factor that determines the aggression level in a child, a link has been found between aggression and smoking. Research reveals that children whose mothers smoked while they were pregnant are showing increased levels of aggression.[1] When this information is coupled with the fact that smoking among girls as young as eleven is on the rise,[2] the need to have effective education on the dangers of smoking is soaring to the top of the charts of public-health priorities.

FASD (fetal alcohol spectrum disorder) is the leading known cause of entirely preventable birth defects and developmental delays in the developed world.[3] Half of the children with FASD will have mental disabilities, and the monetary cost of treating them is estimated to be well above one million dollars per child over the course of his/her lifetime. The human cost of FASD in suffering and lost potential is incalculable.

Babies whose mothers consume significant quantities of alcohol while pregnant are at high risk for FASD. They will sustain damage to their central nervous system, are compromised in terms of normal mental and physical growth, and may have facial abnormalities. The Roots of Empathy instructor discusses FASD frankly with Grade 7 and 8 students, explaining in detail how consumption of alcohol damages the fetus. The alcohol consumed by the mother enters her bloodstream and goes through the placenta into the baby's body. An adult's body is much bigger than the unborn baby's body, which is so tiny at that time that the amount of alcohol it absorbs is far higher, in proportion to its size, than the amount absorbed by its mother. Thus, because the concentration of the alcohol in the baby's body is so high, and because the baby's system is not flushed out as regularly as the mother's body, alcohol stays in the baby for too long, killing brain cells in the process.

Research leaves absolutely no doubt that drinking large amounts of alcohol during pregnancy sentences a baby to a life scarred by learning disabilities, delayed growth, inability to manage anger and a host of other challenges. Children with FASD do not have the language skills, memory, grasp of cause-and-effect thinking, or ability to control their emotions, cope with a regular school environment or establish social relationships. While findings are less conclusive in cases where a pregnant woman's alcohol consumption is very low, the only responsible advice to give is that there is no known safe amount of alcohol that can be consumed during pregnancy. This is the unequivocal message we give to students in Roots of Empathy, and with the older grades we leave posters as visual reminders to reinforce the message.

Never Too Young

Teaching children the messages of safety allows them to understand the protective responsibility of parenthood, the vulnerability of a baby, and the interdependence we need to exercise to make the world safe for all of us. Because issues are approached from an empathic base throughout the program, the focus in the Roots of Empathy curriculum on what it takes to keep a baby safe transfers easily into consideration of the students' own responsibilities in keeping themselves safe. For six-year-olds it may be crossing the street, while for thirteen-year-olds it is lifestyle choices.

For example, a discussion about how the baby's healthy development is linked to good nutrition leads naturally to dealing with a concern about eating habits. In an increasing number of classes, this involves discussion about personal appearance. It is alarming that girls as young as nine years old are developing anxieties about body image. Boys too are no longer immune from this preoccupation. While we establish the vital connection between nourishing food and the optimal growth of the baby's brain and body, we extend it to include the continuing development of young children and adolescents. For issues like body image, dealing with the physical is not enough; the continuous focus on pro-social skills and self-esteem built into every theme and discussion is aimed at providing children with a healthy sense of self and strategies for dealing competently with the maelstrom of social pressures in their environment.

Children worry about many of the same things adults worry about, but do not have the experience to put the worries in context. Ignorance is far from bliss, and the lack of information appropriately shaped and presented by a caring adult can create monster-sized fears for children. Roots of Empathy encourages children to question safety issues that affect them—"Is it okay to . . ? What would happen if . . ?" The process of working out answers together not only adds to their body of knowledge but gives them the confidence to think things through for themselves. When they have information shared in a way they can absorb, children have the tools to put the things that worry them into clearer perspective, make sense of their world and value what keeps them safe.

13

WHAT BABIES
WOULD SAY
TO TEACHERS

Roots of Empathy: The Caring Classroom

I BELIEVE that what we have experienced and discovered in Roots of Empathy programs has profound implications for education. The caring classroom is not only a wonderful place for teachers to work, it is a fruitful and productive learning environment for students.

Reach Me Where I Am

Students are often asked to prove what they know. Roots of Empathy invites them to share what they feel, what they think—in other words, who they are. Each child comes to school as a unique mosaic made up of the values of their families and all the experiences they've had in the preschool years, as well as their genetic inheritance of temperament and talents. To teach children, we must first reach them. Roots of Empathy is designed around the premise that seeing the world from the child's perspective is an essential first step to learning in school. Some children have spent their first four or five years feasting on a banquet of love and enriching experiences. Loving parents have cuddled them, read them stories, sung them nursery rhymes, taken them to the zoo and the park, counted the stairs with them as they carried them up to bed, and encouraged them in their interests, hopes and dreams.

Then there are the not-so-lucky children. Perhaps the child grew up in poverty, whereby hunger was a daily experience and sleep was often interrupted by the sound of family violence. There was no time to read, no money to visit the zoo. Perhaps the child spent the greater part of the day in an unregulated child-care setting, in front of the TV set watching soap operas while a baby cried in the playpen in the corner of the room.

It is obvious that these children, from very different backgrounds, are on different rungs of the ladder when they come to school. The whole concept of public education is that school can provide a new opportunity for those children who are starting out so far behind. Public education is the strongest institution we have for socialization and democracy. For those children who start out with so little, school can mean a better life, and the promise of a future. This makes it all the more important that school systems with a focus on bringing all children to the same level of academic performance at the end of the year have strategies that recognize children's different starting points. Failure to do so puts undue stress on both the child and the teacher. There is a body of thought that pushes for more structure in education, foisting more and more formal instruction on younger children. This is based on the faulty premise that beginning such instruction early trains children to absorb learning at a greater rate as they get older. It flies in the face of all the research about how children really learn. Classroom teachers, particularly at the kindergarten level, often feel they are violating their own values and belief system when they are pushed to substitute instruction for the play-based problem-solving that they know is the foundation of a child's competencies. They worry that play has become a four-letter word and that children's natural learning style, their curiosity and imagination, have been sold out to political decisions based on rhetoric rather than research.

Teachers who have welcomed our program into their classrooms make unanticipated discoveries. As the instructor leads the children in interactions with the Roots of Empathy family, teachers can assume the role of observer of their students and are given a chance to see them in a different light. The observations find their way into the comments on social and emotional learning in the students' report card. More than one teacher has called "Roots" the fourth R. In the development of students' relationship with the baby, teachers often see new behaviour. They may see gentleness, kindness or vulnerability that they rarely see otherwise in some of their students.

A potent example of this is found in the story of Tom, a seven-year-old boy, who had been in and out of foster homes for many years and had exhibited consistently aggressive, anti-social behaviour since the beginning of the school year. He had not been able to make friends and was often very disruptive in class, pushing, hitting, kicking, spitting and punching the other students. He always wore a hat almost covering his eyes and he never smiled.

The teacher was very concerned about having him in class during the Roots of Empathy program in case he might harm the baby. I discussed this with the teacher and the instructor in advance and my advice was to place Tom right next to the baby. The mother and the father both visited with the baby that day. Tom's reactions to the exchanges between the baby and his parents evoked behaviour he had never displayed before. During the first class visit, Tom smiled and interacted with the baby; during the second visit, he took off his hat when he was near the baby; and at the third visit he brought in a bedraggled pink feather to tickle the bottom of the baby's feet. He wanted to bring the baby a present and, having no money, he offered the feather he had found at home. The contact with the baby and the observation of the exchanges between the parents and baby were the key that unlocked his feelings and allowed him to reveal the gentle, sensitive person he was. His teacher and fellow classmates began to see Tom from a new and kinder perspective. The teacher gave him the role of being the lookout at the door to welcome the baby at each visit and help the mother get him out of his stroller. As his emotional literacy grew, so did his belief in himself as a good person and his capacity for empathy. He gradually learned to mix with the children, made friends, and learned to talk about how he was feeling.

Experiences such as this have occurred in many Roots of Empathy classes. Teachers' perceptions of their students' characters expand as they witness them as caring, feeling individuals and learn about their worries and fears. The program reminds teachers how children act out their feelings in their behaviour and that a child's tiresome disruptiveness is often a signal of anxiety and emotional pain. Teachers find that their own empathy for their students deepens. This is often reciprocated as students become aware of the teachers' moments of frustration and offer help.

The milestones that the baby reaches over the year reinforce the students' understanding of the amazing journey of human development and the learnings are levered to allow them to reflect on milestones they themselves are reaching. For adults who feel responsible for helping children attain each milestone safely and competently, the reflections are a reminder of the complex array of skills and social learning that goes into making a fully-fledged, emotionally competent human being. A child is not a soufflé— there is no single moment of evidence to indicate you have failed. A child is a work of art in progress. You may not be able to discern the impact of the contributions you have made to the masterpiece, but they are there in every word of affirmation and encouragement you offer.

The emphasis on the child as a person and on the development of social and emotional competence requires that we allow children to solve problems together, build consensus and be creative. It requires creating a comfort level for them to do so. We concern ourselves less with students' knowledge of facts and more with their ability to solve problems and their growing emotional maturity. Pre-adolescence can be an especially lonely place. Too often, children feel they are islands of emotion. Roots of Empathy is a lifeboat that brings them to a safe and not-so-lonely shore.

All Children Can Be Leaders

When we put children in groupings that are different from their usual classroom grouping, we reshuffle the power structure. Children who previously did not take leadership roles may do so when the structure of the previous grouping is set aside. Many children don't have the confidence to speak out in class in case they make a mistake, or somebody laughs at them. In our format, children have a chance to experience leadership, because they each get a turn to be the group's reporter. When they realize they're not reporting on their own thinking but that of the group, and that they won't be laughed at because it is just not allowed, even the shyest student will try it.

The program also presents to students authentic, real-world problem-solving experiences rather than pencil-and-paper exercises. The problem-solving activities value process over product and encourage creative thinking rather than recollection of facts. We are not dealing with academic materials; instead we are asking students about their personal opinions, about what they feel and who they are. This gives all students, even those normally lacking in self-confidence in regular classes, opportunities for collaborative learning and consensus building. The sense of a caring community within the classroom is considerably strengthened.

A Caring Curriculum

In my description of the Roots of Empathy program earlier in this book, I touched on the fact that it creates multiple links with the regular curriculum. The program's themes sometimes involve students in writing reflective pieces and comments, or in creating poems and stories and then reading them chorally. In terms of music curriculum, they sing and create songs, rewriting nursery rhymes in rap sometimes to illustrate social themes. The mathematics connection comes in when older students are involved with problem-solving as they calculate the expense of diapering their baby, the multiple issues of comfort to the baby, the degree of hassle to the parents, and the environmental impact of disposable over cloth diapers. These exercises also introduce the children to debates about moral issues that are practical and involve multiple perspectives while meeting the challenge of coming to a consensus as a group. And the scientific component is also important: the children discuss the biological aspects of growth and neuroscience when the brain is presented as the pathway to learning, behaviour and health.

Just as the school's curriculum is integrated meaningfully into what is taught in the Roots of Empathy program, so too are there many opportunities to extend what happens in the program to enrich all of the learning that occurs in the school day. The skills children practise in Roots of Empathy group work carry over into positive classroom dynamics and a higher level of comfort in sharing ideas. The excitement generated through experiential learning at the feet of a baby and the sense of family created in the classroom benefit the children, the teacher and the school.

A Grade 1 teacher was teaching a lesson about animals to her class and asked the children to name some animals that laid eggs. Some guessed chickens and sparrows and robins, and Evan who had been to the zoo told the class that snakes laid eggs, too. Then Sienna raised her hand and said, "Dogs lay eggs, too, and then they help the puppies hatch out."

Not the right answer. But the teacher hesitated for a moment to figure out a constructive way to tell Sienna she was wrong. She commented, "I'm wondering if you've seen a dog having puppies." Sienna's face lit up, and she launched into an enthusiastic description of her family's dog, Spud, giving birth to six tiny puppies, each in a small whitish-coloured sac that the little girl described as an egg. "Then Spud licked off the egg and the puppies came out," she concluded, beaming at the teacher and the class.

If she hadn't been attuned to the children's process of exploration, the teacher would have simply told the child that her answer was wrong and gone on to the next waving hand. Sienna would have been frustrated with the teacher. After all, she'd seen those puppies arrive in eggs with her own eyes, hadn't she? If the teacher was wrong about that, how could she be trusted about anything else? She would have been less likely to raise her hand the next time a question was asked. It's embarrassing to be wrong, and frustrating to be told you're wrong when you're convinced that you're right. Deeper than this is the crushed enthusiasm and bruised trust. A child puts her whole vulnerable self out there, expecting the best, trusting that she'll be taken care of. When this doesn't happen, it affects her willingness to venture opinions and her attitude to learning.

And the teacher would have missed the opportunity to clarify the concept she was teaching. She had simply asked about eggs without defining them. And after Sienna's story, the teacher told the class that eggs have hard shells to protect the baby bird or animal inside, and that the puppies were born in sacs, not eggs. Then Evan told the class that he'd touched some snake eggs, and they were sort of soft the way leather feels, not hard like chicken eggs. The teacher had to revise her definition again. Then someone asked about fish eggs, which are also soft and often transparent, and the definition of eggs took on more refinement. Eggs were now understood to be a container.

Because the teacher was empathic not just to the words, but to the tone, the meaning, the excitement born of experience behind a child's response to what seemed like a simple question, a new array of learning possibilities opened up for every child in the classroom. The little girl who had seen the puppies born felt respected, and was able to expand her understanding of what she had observed.

The teacher who is open to the many paths children take in their understanding of the world is able to make the connections between what the child knows already and the new information she is hoping to share. Learning needs something to attach itself to. A piece of information can't stand alone; it needs to fit into the framework of the child's previous experiences and knowledge.

As I have stressed throughout this book, healthy relationships are based on respect. What might this look like in a math class? Let's say the teacher has covered a new math concept, and some of the children are obviously struggling to understand. She could say: "I can see from the looks on your faces that not all of you understood what I was saying. Let me try to explain that in another way. I want us all to get it." She could ask for help from the other students: "I didn't explain that in a way that everyone understood. Would anyone else like to try explaining it in a different way?" She can say, "Some of us got this and some of us didn't. Let's try another approach."

She doesn't name the children whose faces show puzzlement or confusion. She doesn't add, "Well, you weren't paying attention or you would have got it," or "You should have done your homework, then you'd understand this." There should be no shame in not understanding. By handling the situation this way, she is teaching much more than math. These children are gaining respect for different ways of learning and understanding the value of helping and sharing with each other.

Relationship and Learning

The teacher's job is more complex than just imparting knowledge; it has everything to do with establishing the relationships that foster learning. In a deep sense, teaching is a universal parenting activity. Learning is something children can choose to do if we set the scene for them and support them, and this must be done with some attention to the varied ways of learning that exist. The truth is that children are 100 per cent in charge of what they learn.

What makes children decide to learn? One of the most significant factors is the teacher's relationship with the child. Children learn most from human interaction and, within that, learn most from people who have positive regard for them. Think back to your school days. Do you remember the day you learned the five-times table or the day you had to list the causes of the First World War? Or do you remember Miss Reynolds, who encouraged you to join the debating society because you engaged the whole class in arguments about capital punishment? I am willing to bet the dry accumulation of facts has no place in your vibrant memories.

I am equally willing to bet that the teacher who made you believe in yourself, who saw you, liked you, helped you, listened to you, laughed with you, and took you seriously just like your friends do, is the teacher who not only has a special place in your heart, but influenced who you became.

In a society that is increasingly complex and challenging, it is tempting to take the position that the emotional and social life of children in the classroom lies outside the teacher's area of responsibility. This attitude is closely related to the idea that problems can be solved by focusing narrowly on academic testing as a measure of learning and development. These approaches, with their emphasis on instilling particular chunks of information in the child's brain, threaten to reduce the teacher's role to that of a filler-of-empty-buckets. Yet everything we have come to know in recent decades about how the brain grows tells us that this isn't how learning works. The brain is an experience-dependent organ, and the richness of environment is crucial. The learning has to engage the whole child, including her emotions and her social context. The correlation between cognitive skills and social and emotional competence is deep. Studies show that the pro-social skills a child demonstrates in Grade 3 are a stronger predictor of academic success in Grade 8 than the academic achievement attained by that child in Grade 3. [1] The child who is coping with deep emotional pain, who is sad, worried or bullied won't be able to learn, no matter how carefully the lesson plan is crafted or how many pages of homework are handed out.

As we gain a greater understanding of how the human brain works, we are also becoming more aware of the need for connections in learning. Our memory is more like a spider's web than a filing cabinet. Individual scraps of knowledge are linked to others to form complex patterns, each pattern linked to still more data. When we learn something new, our brain's first task is to fit it into the web and determine where it connects. The first time you see a zebra, your brain attaches it to familiar things—"like a horse" you think, and perhaps "uses contrasting colour for camouflage," establishing a link in your mind to animals like leopards and tigers. Get to know a bit more about a zebra, and you might also add it to your list of African animals, now that you know where it lives, and to your mental collection of "animals that look like horses but are not rideable."

But what if you have never seen a horse, not even in a picture? Or know nothing about leopards and tigers and natural camouflage? You may only be able to connect the zebra to "four-legged animals," like cats and dogs, and with only this single, not-very-strong connection, your prospect of truly learning and retaining this new information is slim. Without a wealth of connections on the web, the zebra information is likely to be shunted to the side and eventually lost to memory.

Some children arrive at school with a well-developed network of connections, filled with highways of information, where new learning can be attached and form firm links. They have had opportunities to discover the world in an atmosphere of love and security. Others have had to narrow their brain's pathways into those few learning experiences that seemed essential to their survival, such as how to know when Mommy's getting mad enough to hurt you. The child's energy goes into hyper-vigilance and therefore is not available for learning. Such children have few places to make connections with the new learning we hope to teach them in school.

Teachers open the classroom doors and take whoever comes in. Once the children enter school, teachers need to build on whatever foundation the child arrives with, however shaky and inadequate that foundation is. But passing on isolated facts or information that won't fit into the web of the child's understanding will only leave him more confused. Each new connection you help the child make expands the possibilities for his future learning.

Unique Styles and Teachable Moments

Adding to the challenge, we also know that children learn in different ways. Most teachers know this from their own observations. Sanjay remembers everything you say to him, but even though you tell Jenny twice what her homework is, she's forgotten it completely before she gets home. She needs to write the assignment down on a piece of paper to make sure. Kanchana learns best when she is able to move around—you see her squirming in her seat as she struggles with a math problem. And as Charlie listens to the story you are reading out loud, you notice him doodling little pictures of the main characters on a scrap of paper.

The child who needs to move while learning may be ordered to "Sit still!" and the child who is trying to create images to help him understand may be told, "Stop doodling and pay attention." But these children may be examples of Howard Gardner's "multiple intelligences."[2] Education has traditionally valued the linguistic and logical intelligences but Gardner has built a case for the importance of other types of intelligence including, for example, those he refers to as "bodily-kinesthetic" and "interpersonal." A growing and substantial body of research shows that these ways of learning are innate, and persist throughout a person's lifetime. Ignoring them by teaching in only one style is like putting blindfolds on more than half the students, and then becoming exasperated because they can't see what is written on the board.

Many people think that a quiet classroom is an effective one. The image of twenty-five little heads bent over twenty-five little desks and working away is sometimes thought to present the ideal image of children who are learning. But enthusiasm is noisy and active! Passion for learning is lively! Yes, there will be times when at least some children sit quietly and are absorbed in reading, writing or drawing, but this should not be our goal for meaningful learning in the classroom—especially for younger children, who need to be active and involved with each other. We need to delight in the energy of children.

To preserve that energy, children need to feel safe. They need to feel that the teacher understands them and how they feel, and to trust that they won't be ridiculed for mistakes or treated disrespectfully because they are different from others. Any energy that the child must use to protect herself in the class is not available for learning.

Mary Emming Young of the World Bank writes that "learning begets learning." Experienced teachers understand the value of harnessing the "teachable moment." Many classroom teachers find they are able to extend teachable moments that occur during Roots of Empathy classes into their regular classroom instruction time. In one of our classes Devon, a boy who had considerable learning difficulties, became extremely interested in learning about the baby's milestones, and ate up every piece of information offered. He became an authority on the subject. His classroom teacher, subsequently recognizing a rare "reachable" moment, took him down to the principal, to teach her all about milestones. As a result of this impromptu lesson, Devon was asked to go on the PA system and he became the school's broadcaster of news about the Roots of Empathy baby. Devon's mother made a special trip to the school office to talk about the change in him; he now loved coming to school.

When the lesson is exploration, nobody has to be right 100 per cent of the time, not even the teacher. I remember one child who had grown up in a rural area, with parents who had a deep interest in nature. Adam knew the names of all kinds of plants and trees, and had an intriguing store of information about the natural world. When his class went on a field trip, he was able to point out various plants and tell the other children which ones were poisonous to cows and which ones could grow ten feet tall. The teacher didn't try to redirect the students to something she knew more about; she listened appreciatively and said, "Wow, Adam, I didn't know that. Thanks for telling us." She was honouring individual contributions and including all talents. The students not only learned about the plants in their community, they learned that children can make a contribution and that we can all learn from one another. The flow of learning shouldn't all be one way—from teacher to students. In the most effective classrooms everyone is a learner.

What Teachers Deserve

Every new teacher needs a mentor, someone who can provide guidance in understanding children, especially during the often overwhelming first weeks in the classroom. This mentor needs to be someone who can model empathy for children, and who can help the new teacher see life at school from the child's perspective and explain the many rich facets of the community in which the school is situated. Student teachers need support in learning how to create a safe community in the classroom. Every class and every school should be a participatory democracy in action, where every child is respected and feels that it is safe to ask questions, disagree, speak up and express emotions. That may sound like a tall order, but I know it can be done; we see it every day in our Roots of Empathy classes.

Teaching children is a calling that needs to be imbued with respect for children's interests and individual learning styles, empathy for their emotions, and an understanding of the experiences and history they bring with them into the classrooms. Honouring this calling should inform not only how we train our new teachers but how we support our experienced teachers.

The potential for teachers to make a difference in the lives of children is huge, and it is that potential which has to be nurtured. What we teach in schools can vary according to the mandated curriculum of the current political administration, but who we are and how we relate to children is more powerful than the content of our message. It is the humanizing of the teaching process that sets the conditions for learning that lasts.

What do babies, the babies who one day will walk through your classroom door, have to say to you? "Be the teacher I'll never forget."

14

WHAT BABIES
WOULD SAY
TO PARENTS

The First Relationship

C HILDREN BECOME who they are at home. The relationship between parent and child is the most powerful
relationship under the stars. The loving touch and the
warm voice of a parent are the fuel that fires the growth of a baby's
brain. They are also the safe haven from which he ventures out to
explore the world and give expression to his imagination. Responsiveness to a baby is as essential as the air they breathe. There is no

unimportant day in a child's life; every moment, every conversation, every activity is important. Celebrate each moment, because it is unique and it can't come back. We often mistakenly believe that the big orchestrated occasions like the trip to Disneyland are the landmarks in a child's life. What children carry in their hearts are not events but relationships.It is the giving of ourselves that matters.

When we become parents, we are changed forever. The child who enters our life has an incredible capacity to reach us and inform us. We can become better people because of the pure, protective love our child inspires in us. Becoming a parent makes us raw in every element of emotion and gives us the chance, through our child, to reach unimagined levels of responsiveness and unselfishness. We become fierce and vulnerable, proud and humbled, and we're in it for life.

In return, parents are loved intensely by their young children. It is no accident that the dance of intimacy played out in all our early interactions with our newborn is likened to falling in love. The first relationship—between child and parent—is very much like a passionate love affair. The child cannot bear to be out of sight and touch of the beloved parent. For the child, this is a critical time for nourishing the human need for affiliation. When this early need for attachment is met fully and lovingly, a child develops securely into an adult with the capacity to self-replenish. When our need for connection is not met, we are forever searching for love or security or approval and we never feel filled up.

The natural milestones of life mitigate the intensity of this first love. As children move on to play groups and child care and school, new relationships with other children and significant adults develop. As children form new friendships, there are peaceful pauses and healthy spaces in the parent–child relationship. The need for approval and love no longer lies 100 per cent with the parent, but begins to be shared through the broader social network that is being developed.

Learning in the Early Years

Roots of Empathy evolved from years of experiencing directly the astonishing influence of loving, engaged parenting, not only on children's social and emotional competence but on their readiness to learn. What we have learned from the last few decades of neuroscience and child-development research shines a light on the early years as a pivotal period with exquisite learning opportunities that are unparalleled in the balance of a lifetime. The nurturance of a loving adult does more to foster intellectual competence than any course or program or teacher.

The lessons of neuroscience fill parents with excitement and an awesome sense of responsibility as they consider their role in the "wiring" of the basic architecture of their baby's brain. The development of the baby's brain hinges on a complex interplay between the genes she was born with and the experiences her parents surround her with. In the first three years of her life, in particular, there are critical periods during which her brain is "wired" through the sensing pathways of touch, vision, hearing, taste and smell.

This knowledge is empowering for parents. Every small act takes on meaning in terms of the capacities they are helping their child to develop. Holding a newborn closely, gently stroking him as he is being fed, singing to him as you rock him in your arms— all these interactions fill him with a range of sensory stimuli that build a sense of security that will shape his capacity to establish warm, healthy relationships for the rest of his life. Every time you respond to his cries of distress and hunger, you are relaying to him a sense of efficacy. He connects the cries he initiates with the comfort that follows, confirming for him that he can influence his world. When you play peekaboo, you are doing more than eliciting delightful giggles; you are helping your child make the transition to understanding that objects are permanent whether he can see them or not; you are teaching him that when you hide something, it can reappear. This is the dawning of memory and the beginning of cause-and-effect thinking.

Probably more than anything else, reading with your child has a lasting impact on her sense of confidence and love of learning. Cuddling your child on your lap as you read a story together is a total sensory experience—the loving warmth of your arms, the rhythmic sound of your voice, the visual stimulation of the story-book pictures, the extended mental imagery as you discuss what is happening. It is no wonder that the level of language development of children who have been frequently read to is markedly greater than for children who have little or no experience of early reading. Children absorb our loves and interests. Just as important as reading to your child is modelling your own personal love of reading. Aside from the known benefits of language acquisition, there is also recent research that links a parent's engagement in reading to a child to positive effects on pro-social behaviour. [1]

Babies who are spoken to get a sense of what language is all about long before they recognize words. Babies a year and under can understand a great deal more than they can say. Before they speak, babies build a huge store of knowledge about speech and language. It is crucial for parents to talk to their baby. Babies learn the sound and cadence of the language that will be theirs. More importantly, they learn that they are able to engage the parent in conversation. They learn the turn-taking of interacting through conversation. Babies will naturally start babbling. When parents respond to the babble, they are encouraging the baby to repeat those utterances. If you reward them by repeating what they have said, they will extend the utterances and take turns with you in conversation. The "two-step" of communication is called that because it really is about being in step with the person you're speaking to. The key to sharing language with babies is that the language must always be tied to the ongoing events in the baby's life—it must be tied to context. It is meaningful when you put on a baby's hat and say the word "hat." The baby's first words are usually the names of people and things that have immediacy to her, the people who love and take care of her and the things in her world of which she has an image.

When we talk to babies, we find ourselves speaking in a high-pitched voice, enunciating slowly, and repeating sounds and phrases in a singsong way. This "parentese," or "baby talk," has gone in and out of vogue over the decades. It is currently "in" because advancements in technology have allowed us to see how babies respond quite differently to parentese versus regular speech patterns. The tone and style of parentese helps babies learn language because it concentrates on vowels, repeats words, and pauses between words to give babies a chance to hear the sounds of the language. The almost melodic fluctuation in cadence and the exaggerated vowel sounds are magical connections to babies. They pay attention longer and more acutely to parentese than to regular speech. Also, causality is much better learned through emotion: a baby learns that when she says *agoo*, the parent will say it back. Language is not strictly an exchange of sound; it is an exchange of emotion paired with sound. Parentese delivers sound through love rather than logic, and makes communication a rich emotional experience.

The frequency with which an adult talks with children and the cumulative impact of this talk make up the advantages or disadvantages a child has on entering school. Although it is more likely that the frequency and complexity of conversations with young children will be less in homes at the lower end of the socioeconomic scale, it is a deficit that can be turned around by programs such as parenting centres, where parents are coached in talking with their children as they engage in play-based activities. When one considers that the language a child learns by age three sets her on a trajectory for success in school, it is all the more pressing that we strive to make optimal early language acquisition a reality across the socio-economic spectrum. Language and cognitive skills are inextricably linked. As soon as babies are able to form mental images of their world, they are on the road to higher-level thinking.

Shaping Character: The Development of Empathy

Not only language but culture and values are formed in the early years in the home. Parenting style has a dramatic effect on who a child becomes. Self-confident, empathic and socially competent children are children who have been raised by parents who are warm and responsive. Authoritative rather than authoritarian, they set limits but give reasons. Authoritative parents monitor their children's behaviour and activities but also involve them in decision-making. They encourage discussion and offer options. Most of all, they walk the talk and model the behaviour they are encouraging in their children.

Nancy Eisenberg, in her book *The Caring Child*, refers to the work of Samuel and Pearl Oliner, who studied people living in Europe during the era of Nazi domination, and examined the factors that had an effect on whether people actively helped Jews to escape or avoided becoming involved. A clear picture emerged of the relationship the helpers had with their parents. "Parents of rescuers, more than parents of bystanders, tended to emphasize caring and the application of ethical obligations to all people, reasoned with the children in disciplinary encounters, and used relatively little physical punishment. Parents of rescuers also modeled caring behaviour in their interactions with people outside the family, as well as in the way in which they administered discipline and punishment."[2]

When parents entrust their children to the school system, they expect that the learning and character-shaping experiences their children have at school will build on the strong foundation provided in the home. They expect to enter into a partnership that will enable their children to be the caring citizens and competent parents of the next generation.

Roots of Empathy works with schools to meet those expectations. The program was born out of a deep concern for the personal and societal values of the next generation and for how these are influenced by the quality of parenting children receive. The wonderful start in life described in this chapter so far is sadly not the lot of all children. Many children come to school from homes where their early experiences have failed to encourage their potential or nourish their souls; they are yet another generation of victims in a continuous cycle of transmission of insensitive, neglectful or even abusive parenting. One of the goals of Roots of Empathy is to break that cycle, so that all children have the experience of a working model of a loving, nurturing parent–child relationship. There is great strength in having the parent and baby visit over an entire year. The children are experiencing the parent–child interaction in multiple situations; they are coached to take charge of the dialogue that occurs in the classroom. There is no stress for them, no exam—they are assimilating for a lifetime the model of a positive empathic relationship.

We know from their work and their insights over the program year that the children in our classes are internalizing the lessons. The social experiences sink under their skin. They can see the milestones of the first year of life and the amazing learning unfolding in the baby's brain under the loving touch of her parent. They learn the amount of care and protection and attention to safety required to bring a baby happily and successfully through her first year. They hear first-hand from the baby's parents about the work and responsibility and sleepless nights that go along with the thrills and discoveries.

Observation of the flow of connection between parent and baby, how the baby sends signals about his needs and how the parents read these cues and respond to them, leads naturally into consideration of the emotions involved. What does sad look like? How do you know when someone is upset or angry? Why do you think the baby is proud? What kinds of things make you feel proud? The exchange of perceptions allows the class to see the many ways people experience happiness or sadness and to refine for themselves the nuances of their feelings. The discussion moves on to exploring the concept of understanding how another person might feel if, for example, she lost her tooth or was being ignored in the schoolyard. This move into taking the perspective of the other person is the crucial step to trying on someone else's feelings and developing empathy for what that person is experiencing. The next crucial step is this: What can you do about it?

At this point empathy becomes a springboard for civic spirit, social action and altruism. Children are gifted in the range of solutions they bring to problems of isolation or sadness or bullying. Their responses go beyond saying "I'm sorry you're sad." In writing about a picture of a crying girl, a Grade 4 student says, "This person might be sad because her friends have left her out of something she wanted to do." In the next sentence she adds, "I would help this person by inviting her to play with me and make sure she has a good time." In many schools, the Roots of Empathy students are recognized as the peacemakers, the ones who intervene in schoolyard conflicts and talk through solutions.

I believe that in addition to their child's achievements in reading, writing and arithmetic, parents want to see growth and development in social confidence, empathy, and they want to see their child becoming a voice for social justice. Towards the end of the Roots of Empathy year, there is a theme called Who Am I? For the students in Grades 7 and 8, this is a time to think about the hopes and dreams they have for themselves. They have been learning about responsibility to a baby. They now extend that thinking to the baby's place in the world, and to how, as citizens of the community and of the globe, we have responsibilities to ensure that all babies, like their Roots of Empathy baby, have a safe, equitable and healthy environment in which to grow. Students learn that they can be change-makers. They can stand up to bullies, not just on their own behalf but in support of their friends; they can articulate what they believe in. The caring community they have helped to build in the classroom is the backdrop to their vision of themselves as people who can make a difference.

You Are the Expert

A child's passage from helpless newborn to confident adult is profoundly influenced by his parents, who are his first love and his first and most powerful teachers. We need to struggle against the pressures that threaten our intuitive parenting and push us to hand our power over to "experts." In an age of instant feedback and the disappearance of the extended family, we are at risk of relying on remote gurus to guide us in child rearing. But there are no one-size-fits-all formulae; what works has everything to do with the context of the relationship. We need to trust ourselves. The philosopher and poet George Santayana wrote, "It is wisdom to believe the heart." Experts have useful information to share but, ultimately, it is the conviction we feel in our heart that will guide us in deciding what is right for our own children.

Roots of Empathy offers children hope as well as skills. In celebrating parenting we are acknowledging that the highest qualities of humanity are played out in the parent–child relationship. In exploring these qualities with children, we are helping them build sustainable self-knowledge and the confidence to take on effectively all the relationships and roles life has to offer. We want to ensure that all the knowledge, gifts, energy and love you invest in being a parent is transferred to the next generation.

In our classroom, we often ask, "If the baby could talk, what would she say?" Maybe she is saying: "When you 'baby talk' with me, I hear a learning song. When you cuddle me, I know I have a safe place in the world. When you pick me up each time I cry, I learn I can talk to you and you will listen. When I point at things and you give me words for them, language is dancing into shape in my mind. When you place a toy for me to reach out to, you teach me how to manage my world."

Babies grow into insightful Grade 7 boys like Jett Allen Estey, who wrote:

Babies

Babies are angels that fly to earth
Their wings disappear at the time of birth
One look in their eyes and we're never the same
They're part of us now and that part has a name
That part is your heart and a bond that won't sever
Our babies are angels, we love them forever

15

CHANGING
THE WORLD
CHILD BY CHILD

and it makes me Happy

My Heart

The Way of the Heart

ROOTS OF EMPATHY, in all the many ways it works in the classroom and beyond, is grounded in respect for the empathic ethics and social genius of young children. These qualities shine through their art—the poetry of their soul—to illuminate the human values we seek to preserve and grow in a world where the promise of a civil society is yet to be fulfilled.

Centuries of philosophy, social reform, intellectual investigation, medical advances and explosions in knowledge about human development continue to run parallel to war, civil conflict, famine, disease and poverty. I remember when we first saw images of Earth from space and were overawed by the beautiful planet we live on. There are days when the weight of human suffering distorts those images into one of a globe covered with open wounds. Where are the lasting solutions? I believe it will take nothing less than a revolution of the human heart to heal those wounds, to make us whole.

We must go back to the beginning and start with the children. In Roots of Empathy we start with the littlest child—a baby two or three months in the world. When this baby smiles into the face of the class's "problem kid," a girl whose behaviour has drawn only stern responses from the teacher and avoidance from her classmates, we see a remarkable thing happen. The girl, seeing only acceptance, smiles back; she says the baby's name in a tone of voice no one in the room has heard before. A desire to connect is apparent in her every movement. I think it is about the beginning of healing in a wounded heart. It is the response of a child who has been trapped in a frightening cycle of punishment–bad behaviour–punishment and who for the first time in a long time encounters a pure smile, unquestioning affection. Somebody likes her. The vista of hope this opens up is one of the small miracles that occur again and again in the Roots of Empathy program. The initial connection between the troubled girl and the baby grows into new perceptions for the other children and the teacher, perceptions of the gentle heart inside the troubled and troublesome child. The common thread of relating to the baby outweighs the earlier sense of alienation. The seeds of community are sown in the classroom.

Far too many people in the world are emotional islands, cut off from meaningful connection to others because they can't speak the universal language of their emotions. Roots of Empathy is the universal language we have all been looking for. It actively teaches emotional literacy, so that every student will be able to understand, name and discuss his own emotions and those of others. Emotional literacy is the first and most important literacy in life. Children who are able to express their feelings and understand the emotional expression of others are equipped with a social competence that eases the formation of friendships and satisfactory relationships with adults. Social and emotional learning requires the use of higher-level thinking skills and is strongly correlated to cognitive learning. This interweaving of competencies makes a powerful case for integrating the development of empathy into the life of school classrooms. A growing mountain of research supports this integration as having a strong effect on children's sense of self, on their engaging in cooperative, helping behaviours and resisting aggression as a way to achieve goals or resolve conflict. The sustainable self-esteem that emerges is not the pop-psych of the 1970s and 1980s, the "tell yourself you're great and you are" kind; it is an internal compass that can reinforce values and guide decisions.

Living by What We Know

The interdependence engendered by this kind of learning is precisely what the global family is sorely in need of. We need to live by what we have come to know. It is not enough to understand intellectually that destruction of the rain forests has a devastating effect on the ozone layer and therefore the future of the planet. We have to translate the understanding into action, recognize the interdependence of trees, ozone and human life in order to stop destroying the rain forests. It is not enough to *know* that the sustained and loving engagement of parents is the single most influential factor on the healthy growth of the human child and if that knowledge is not acted on—if we continue to leave parents, especially the most vulnerable of them, to struggle alone without the supports and resources they need to give their child a healthy start in life. We have to stop the rhetoric and do the things that *will* put children first. We need to honour parents and recognize the interdependence between family-friendly societies, competent parenting and healthy, confident children. It is not enough to know that the age-old resorting to armed aggression, bombing or starving our perceived opponent into submission resolves nothing and only breeds further conflict as the effects spill over from nation to nation. We have to recognize that ultimately we are dependent on one another, that when one nation loses we all lose, and that what we particularly lose is another piece of our humanity, our progress towards civilization. We are borrowing the future from our children, and we have to ensure that what we do today does not diminish but instead enriches the world we will leave to them—and their children.

Imagine the Roots of Empathy effect in a global context. Imagine what it would mean if the attunement that informs the loving, learning relationship between parent and baby were translated into all human relationships, if each person's expressions of emotion and need were met by caring, empathic responses. We know that ideally a child is loved into being a loving person at home. When school becomes the next significant influence, we need a school culture that fosters social trust and respect. And if children were not loved into being loving at home, can they learn to be caring at school? Yes, they can and, when we consider the implications for health, well-being and competence over their life span, they must be. Providing them with this opportunity is the only responsible thing to do.

As a society we have an obligation to ensure that when parents, for whatever reason, are unable to provide a model of warm, responsive parenting, this deficit does not become the destiny of their children. It is not useful to blame and shame adults for deficits in parenting that they inherited. It is constructive to help parents to take responsibility in their parenting by providing the supports that are required. We have an obligation to halt the cycle, to give every child an alternative and to open the door to caring and trust for them, so that when they become parents they will not be doomed to pass on to their children the harsh beginning they experienced themselves. We also seek to develop the sense of social justice that will encourage them as adults, whether or not they become parents themselves, to build a society that is a model of interdependence and inclusion.

Imagine a generation of children across the world entering into adulthood and parenthood armed with self-esteem, a reciprocity of understanding of emotions, a sense of community, a commitment to peaceful resolution of conflict, a valuing of social inclusion. Imagine the world this would call into being:

- Every child raised on a banquet of love in a society where their parents are not penalized in terms of income, opportunity or self-development for the act of becoming a parent.
- Every school a centre of collaborative learning that trains the heart as well as the mind, where character and intelligence are equally valued and nourished, where we celebrate helpfulness, cooperation and kindness as well as good math scores.
- Every community a place of human connection, where social trust exists, where no one is left to struggle in poverty or neglect or isolation.
- Every nation a peaceful member of an interdependent global family, where the valuing of human life and the protection of our environment are the yardsticks by which all decisions are measured.

These are not new values or ideals. As long as there has been strife and hunger and exploitation and cruelty, there have been visionaries, humanitarians and people of goodwill who have advocated another life-affirming way. What *is* new is that we no longer have an excuse to go on inflicting pain and dividing up the earth's resources as if the world were still a collectivity of medieval fiefdoms separated from one another by impassable mountain ranges and unknown seas. We know too much. At the touch of a button, we can see children dying from disease and famine, while we know that the medicine and food that would save them exists. At the touch of a button we can see the victims of war and poverty, with hopelessness and suffering, while political leaders feed us what we know is diversionary rhetoric about balancing budgets and balancing power. At the touch of a button we can visit the devastation of a country five thousand miles away or the mean streets of our own troubled cities where children are hounded by bullies. Where, in all the gadgetry of our lives, is the "empathy button"? Where is the on switch of human responsibility that would let us feel the emotion behind what we know and impel us to stand up and take action for what we believe in?

We know that the ability to express emotion, the ability to understand another's point of view and the ability to respond empathically to the expressed emotions of others is the currency of relationship-building. We know that these skills are learned and that empathy can be developed. Even though the ideal environment for this learning is the early years, we know that it is not too late to open doors to emotional literacy and empathy in the school years. We know that even for children who have a solid start in life, nourishing emotional literacy and empathy through the school years strengthens social competence and altruistic behaviours. [1]

Making It Happen

Roots of Empathy takes this knowledge beyond an interesting topic of research and makes it a concrete experience for children.

It speaks to the affective, or caring, side of the child and takes the live and in-colour model of an infant–parent relationship into the classroom. A year of observation, interaction and human-development activities brings to life for these children, beyond the power of any textbook or screen, the dynamic growth of the body, the mind and the heart of a baby. The baby's human-development story is partnered with learning about the influence and responsibility of being a parent and it is a springboard for children to consider their own human development. The anecdotal and research evidence emerging from our program paints a picture of change both at the classroom level and in the individual child. Children are articulating a concept of themselves as complex human beings with valid feelings and a sense of intrinsic pride. In the Roots of Empathy program, children achieve deep levels of self-reflection as they are encouraged to identify personal situations in which they themselves were able to do something that made them feel proud of their character, regardless of how invisible the act may have been to others. Children in our classes have talked about pride in terms of their refusal to join friends engaging in risky behaviour even though it might have excluded them from the "in" group, or their persistence in wearing detested braces because it meant keeping a promise to oneself. This kind of intrinsic pride is a deep, healthy and long-lasting alternative to the fleeting accolades that come from activities recognized extrinsically, through trophies or the praise of others. The kind of pride we work to cultivate is connected to sustainable self-confidence, addresses character and adds positively to the image of self a child carries into adulthood.

At the classroom level, Roots of Empathy is achieving the characteristics of a caring community. The concept of intrinsic pride is connected to reflections and discussions children have as the Roots of Empathy year draws to a close. The theme Who Am I? asks children to write a letter about themselves to the baby that begins with the words "I am important because . . ." In one class, a Grade 2 boy started to cry and said, "I'm not good at anything!" He was immediately surrounded by his classmates, who not only consoled him but talked to him about all the things he was good at, from making the baby laugh to being a reading buddy to the kindergarten kids. The children had specific things to offer this boy, but even when there is no ready solution, it is the reaching out and connection to another's pain that matters most. Responsiveness to the anxieties of others and care taken to make everyone feel included and valued are aspects of the human connections that deepen over the school year.

I have described how the end-of-year wishes the children make for their baby take them beyond empathy to active thinking and planning for another person's well-being and happiness; these wishes put them on the road to altruism. The concrete ties they have developed with the baby connect children in a more substantial way with the future they are imagining. When they are treated as thinking citizens and active stakeholders in their future, their capacity to see themselves as people who can change their world and who can challenge injustice and cruelty is heightened. The seeds that grow into altruistic behaviour are planted.

The journey the Roots of Empathy children take over the school year brings them to a place not only where others see them, but where they see themselves as reflective, thinking, altruistic, responsible, caring and empathic people. In their wishes for the baby, they do what they do best: they dream. We may be lucky enough to inhabit the world they imagine.

Child by Child

Musical chairs. Snakes and Ladders. It is telling that these popular childhood games have a viciousness built into them, a viciousness that reflects what is wrong with our society. The music plays, the music stops, and if you can't keep up you are excluded, you're out of the game. A roll of the dice determines whether you climb up the ladder or tumble down the snake. There is only one winner; everyone else loses. Think of how many families are left without a refuge in the musical chairs of life. Think of the babies who are born into advantage that assures them a place at the top of the ladder, while so many others are threatened with a slide down the snake.

It is time to abandon the old games and create a game that is fair, where no one loses. Roots of Empathy argues against the simplistic approach of a competitive world. Children learn that no one person has all the answers and there are no simple solutions. They learn that the best outcomes are achieved when everyone is given a voice and when everyone opens their minds and hearts to listen to others' voices. This lesson of respect teaches that one's own satisfaction in life is contingent on ensuring that a satisfying life is within everyone's reach. The children in Roots of Empathy learn that heartwork is as vital as brainwork. More importantly, they learn that without the heartwork, the value of the brainwork is diminished. At the level of the classroom, they are learning what has yet to be assimilated by nations: that no conflict has ever been resolved by reason or intellect alone. It takes the reason of the mind and the wisdom of the heart to create peace and understanding.

Roots of Empathy children are storing up skills to create a generation of parents and citizens who will change the world, child by child.

APPENDIX A

THE STORY OF PARENTING
AND FAMILY LITERACY CENTRES

VERY EARLY IN MY CAREER as a kindergarten teacher I came to a sharp realization: that by the time children start school, their concept of themselves is already formed. To a large extent their experiences in their earliest years set them on a trajectory for success or failure. The home has a profound impact on the child's attitude to learning and his sense of competence. The relationship between the child and the parent is the most powerful teaching relationship there is. The quality of nurturing from a caring adult in these first critical years has a profound impact on readiness to learn and the capacity to form strong healthy relationships and hence the child's future success in school and in life.

In 1981, armed with these insights, I initiated parenting and family literacy centres in a handful of Toronto schools. The Toronto Board of Education funded these centres because they shared my concern about the high rate of school dropouts, teen pregnancy and academic failure experienced by children in the poor inner-city communities. The centres were set up in a classroom, or in some cases a double classroom, to welcome parents and their babies or preschool-aged children. The idea was to invite parents to identify what help they needed in dealing with the problems in their lives, rather than telling them what they needed to work on. All of the centres were in low-income areas that had more than their fair share of drugs, prostitution and crime and less than their fair share of parks and community resources. Community starts to really matter to the child when she is about four years old, but community matters hugely to the parent right from the start, particularly one who is raising a child on one's own, in poverty, or without the ability to speak English.

The centres worked on a drop-in basis. Families could come four days a week and in some cases on Saturdays. Unlike many programs for parents and preschoolers, this program kept the parent and child together all the time. The parenting agenda was addressed directly by teaching parents, in a playful way, what was normal or typical development and behaviour. There was only one staff person per centre, a parent worker who was responsible for the early child development program, parent support and education, the resource program, the book and toy libraries, community outreach and the nutrition program. This worked like a symphony as all of the parents, grandparents and care-givers felt it was their program and were delighted to contribute. I used to measure group cohesiveness in the spontaneous way that people helped when there was a need—wiped other children's noses, changed the diaper of babies other than their own and intervened in child-to-child conflict. The parent worker would sit down on the floor with the parents and explain what was hap-pening developmentally with their child. For example, if a baby was banging things and irritating the parent, the parent worker could explain that, at about nine months, children develop the skill of being able to hammer intentionally. They get quite excited about this new power and will hammer anything in sight with any object they find. The parent would be offered the hammer-and-peg set to take home from the toy lending library we had set up, so that the child could practise the new skill, and the parent could be proud of the new milestone in the child's development. Parents passed on this kind of information to one another. We avoided parenting classes that involved handouts and formal instruction. Instead, a great deal of discussion took place informally around the painting easel and sandbox. Parents would be greatly relieved to hear, for example, that it is not in the nature of a two-year-old to share.

The "411" Approach

Parents are naturally loath to attend programs that tell them "how to be a good parent." The parenting program we initiated came from a different premise, from a position of respect for parents and a belief that they want to do their best for their children. The parents we began with were seen as having strengths and experiences they could share with one another. The worker in the parenting centre was a facilitator and a catalyst. At that time, most other programs started with the assumption that they were there to fix a deficit. Their message was that parents were failing, and the program had an expert who would provide all the answers to their problems. I believed strongly in taking a "resource-based" or "411" rather than an "emergency rescue" or "911" approach. A "911" approach is about rescuing, reclaiming, recovering—after the damage is done—and it inevitably falls far short of the mark. Why else would an economically advanced country like Canada incarcerate more young people than any other developed country?[1] In building on the strengths of parents and children, and opening doors to self-awareness and a sense of efficacy through literacy of language and literacy of feelings, we can develop social and emotional competencies that break patterns of human suffering—a "411" approach: a resource, not a rescue mission. The philosophy underlying our parenting programs was preventative.

In welcoming parents to the centres, the parent worker did not present them with forms or bureaucratic hoops to jump through. Conversations were aimed at quickly discovering what kind of safety net people had and what kind of friendly supports, if any, they had in their lives. We would ask questions such as "When you are ill or your child is ill, where do you turn for help?" The answers allowed us to see whether the parent needed to be connected with helpful neighbours in the community. In communicating to parents the importance of their voice and the scope for them to have a meaningful role in the centre, we would ask: "How can you help us set up this centre in a way that will work for you?" "How can I help you?" "If there were things you would like to change about your life, what would they be?" "What do you hope for your child?" The dialogue this created went a long way to establishing trusting relationships and a fertile ground for parents making a difference together.

These centres supported parents in learning the literacy and mathematical concepts their children needed to be successful in kindergarten. This learning took place as the parent worker modelled informally for the parents the kind of conversations that might take place when they were playing with their child and how they could use these conversations to encourage language development and reinforce concepts. Parents were coached in what I called a "play-based, problem-solving" curriculum. They learned playful ways to have meaningful conversations as they played with their preschoolers, capitalizing on the power of their relationship to build vocabulary, curiosity and imagination. Parents in communities dense with tall apartment buildings learned that if they got out of the elevator one floor before their own, they could count each step they climbed. They learned the ways that little children learn—through love and encouragement and meaningful play, not through instruction.

Empathic Outreach

One of the schools selected for a parenting centre was in Canada's first post–World War II housing project, Regent Park. In this school, the focus was on setting up a parenting centre exclusively for teenage mothers. Society has been quick to criticize these young parents when they run into problems. But we criticize them from a perspective that doesn't understand the burden of poverty on young shoulders. We don't appreciate what it takes for that mother to push her child in a stroller with one wheel broken, dragging a bag of laundry along with her, waiting in the laundromat while the damp clothes dry so that they won't be stolen and, at the same time, trying to entertain a cranky toddler. When she "loses it," we don't realize the effort it took for her to keep things together for so long. Many of these mothers are heroes, but they aren't recognized as such. These were the mothers I wanted to work with, offering them a place of encouragement and support through the parenting centres.

Young mothers who had been criticized at every turn saw an invitation to the program not as medicine to fix what was wrong with them but as a welcome to a place of trust where they were respected. Although the program offered universal access, in the first year of outreach we also targeted families who would not normally elect to attend, families who struggled with addiction, domestic violence and child abuse, families who needed a supportive, non-judgmental community group where they felt they could belong. Sometimes this meant the centre became the venue for supervised access to allow a mother just released from jail to reconnect with her children. As these parents became integrated into the life of the parenting centres and grew in competence and self-respect, I saw the dawning of real hope.

The theme of empathy drove my outreach to these young women. In order to reach them, I needed to understand their perspective and I needed to demonstrate that I cared. Some were very young girls who had dropped out of school to have their babies, and persuading them to walk through the doors of that building again was not an easy task. Most had negative memories of school and an overarching sense of failure. My first approach was to borrow a friend's baby and to wear that baby in a Snugli as I lined up in the bank on welfare-cheque day. Each time a young mother came in, I chatted with her about the program and told her when the parenting centre would be opening. Putting myself in the young mother's shoes as she cashed her cheque, I realized that the money meant that clothes could be washed, food could be bought, and there would still be enough to celebrate with fries and gravy. On other days, I wore the baby to the laundry rooms in the apartment buildings and spent time talking to the young women as they waited for their clothes. I carried a bubble-making liquid to attract the babies of the young women and scented playdough for their toddlers. A mother of any age appreciates someone who plays with her children and is more likely to trust another woman with a baby.

I also had a camera and offered to take a Polaroid picture of the young mother's baby, knowing that mothers of all ages treasure a baby picture. I would give the print to the mother and take another photo, this time offering to make a nine-by-twelve blow-up. I told the mom she could pick it up at the parenting centre in the school, which was so close I could point to it. These teen moms came to the program to claim the baby's picture, and we had a high-school film club who came to do family portraits. None of the moms turned it down. They stayed for lunch—and then they stayed, on average, six years, bound by their common experience.

This face-to-face outreach is not transferable to a hired out-reach worker who has no role in the centre itself; vulnerable mothers will chance coming out to a program if they have a sense of trust that the person who invited them genuinely wants them to come.

Building School–Community Relationships

A central idea behind the centres was that if parents received support in their parenting and encouragement in learning with their children before the children entered kindergarten, we might be able to start the children off on a strong footing and engage the parents positively in the children's school life. The partnership that developed between parenting centres and schools went a long way towards demystifying the school system for parents who had no confidence in their place there. Parents became comfortable interacting with the school staff and built up skills in advocating for their children's learning. When children who came to the parenting centre saw their parents engaged in conversation with the principal in the hallway, they felt that the school was theirs and they belonged there. As parents' skills in play-based learning activities grew, we trained them to volunteer in the school kindergarten classes. This was a boon in situations where the parent spoke the language of a child newly arrived in the country. The volunteer parent was able to talk to the teacher about the child's competencies and be a support to the teacher in helping the child progress rapidly.

In one community, where both parents had to go out to work, grandmothers looked after the children. This was predominantly a Portuguese community with two or even three branches of the extended family sharing a house. The grandmothers, dressed in black, brought the babies and toddlers of their adult children to the parenting centre. These women had immigrated to Toronto with low levels of literacy in their mother tongue. We had Portuguese versions of storybooks that had one line of story to the page. The Board of Education paid for a literacy instructor to teach the grandmothers to read in Portuguese. The result for the children was experience with early literacy in the form of bedtime stories, in their mother tongue, on the laps of their grandmothers. The result for the grandmothers was a confidence that led them to form the first home and school association the school had ever had. The inaugural meeting was run in Portuguese with an interpreter hired by the principal for the English-speaking school staff. These women, whose sphere of influence had largely been in the kitchen, were now participating in decisions—made all in Portuguese—about the equipment that would go in the school playground, the hours the library would be open, and whether the school would be able to hire a music teacher. The positive implications for the kind of start their grandchildren got in school were profound. The big bonus to the school system was their new understanding of the cultures of the community and a growing sense of the contribution families make to their child's development. This mutuality went a long way to breaking down the barriers between home and school.

Parenting and School Readiness

Research undertaken by the school board confirmed unequivocally that we more than met the goal that was the original driving force behind the establishment of the parenting centres—changing academic outcomes of inner-city children by increasing readiness levels and involving parents with the school. The literacy level of the immigrant children in the centres, when tested at school entry, was dramatically higher than the levels of their neighbours who didn't attend the parenting centres.

These were the first school-based parenting and family literacy centres in Canada, and today they represent the largest school-based program of this kind in the country. Their success led to their proliferation. By 2004, centres existed in fifty-four schools with more than 12,000 children and 8,000 families participating. Most are in communities where a high proportion of the families come from a variety of language and cultural backgrounds and are economically disadvantaged. More than 60 per cent of the families do not speak English at home. Nonetheless, when it is time to start school these children are ready to take advantage of the learning that school has to offer and schools are more ready to receive the children.

APPENDIX B

EFFECTIVENESS OF "THE ROOTS OF EMPATHY" PROGRAM IN PROMOTING CHILDREN'S EMOTIONAL AND SOCIAL COMPETENCE:

A Summary of Research Outcome Findings

by Kimberly A. Schonert-Reichl, Ph.D.,
University of British Columbia

Introduction

CAN AN INFANT be a catalyst for change? More specifically, is the "Roots of Empathy" (ROE) program effective in promoting children's social emotional competence and reducing their aggressive behaviours? This is the question that we at the University of British Columbia have tried to answer during the past four years. Beginning in 2000 we conducted a series of investigations aimed at discerning the effectiveness of the ROE program on children's social and emotional competence. The following is a summary of what we have found so far. First, we outline the rationale for promoting children's social and emotional competence in schools.

Background: The Case for Promoting
Social–Emotional Competence in Schools

A growing segment of school-age children experience or are at risk for a myriad of psychological and behavioural problems that interfere with their interpersonal relationships, successful school performance and potential to become productive contributing citizens (see, for example, Canadian Education Statistics Council, 2000; OECD, 1995; Steinhauer, 1996). Epidemiological reports of prevalence rates of disorder are in accord in suggesting that approximately one in five children and adolescents experiences mental health problems severe enough to warrant treatment by mental health services (National Advisory Mental Health Council, 1990; Offer & Schonert-Reichl, 1992; Offord, Boyle, & Racine, 1991; Romano, Tremblay, Vitaro, Zoccolillo, & Pagani, 2001). Childhood aggression, in particular, has been identified as a salient concern by researchers, clinicians and educators alike, not only because of continuities in the manifestation of aggressive behaviours in children (Farrington, 1992; Loeber, Wung, Keenan, & Giroux, 1993; Patterson, 1993) and concomitant problems associated with childhood aggression such as peer rejection and hyperactivity (Coie & Dodge, 1998; Parke & Slaby, 1983), but also because the behaviours in which aggressive children engage are often associated with significant disruption to the social and academic ethos for other children in classrooms and schools as well as the community at large. Because early aggressive behaviour is the single best predictor of delinquency and later aggression (Farrington, 1991), such behaviours have emerged as a target for early prevention and intervention efforts in schools with the rationale that such programs may be more effective in reducing antisocial and aggressive behaviours than later treatment or penalties (Institute of Medicine, 1994; Offord et al., 1991).

Over the past few decades, researchers have identified a number of factors that significantly increase the likelihood of an upward trajectory of aggressive behaviours. Most notably, the potent role that social–emotional understanding plays in determining children's present and future adjustment has risen to prominence in recent years (Battistich, Solomon, Watson, & Schaps, 1997; Cook, Greenberg, & Kusche, 1994; Dodge & Coie, 1987; Eisenberg & Miller, 1987; Miller & Eisenberg, 1988; Schonert-Reichl, 1993). One dimension of social–emotional understanding that has been given increased attention in recent years is that of empathy. Empathy, defined here as an individual's emotional responsiveness to the emotional experiences of another, is increasingly being recognized as an important dimension of social competence because it not only tends to prompt altruistic behaviours (Eisenberg & Miller, 1987; Hoffman, 1981), but because it also "may play a particularly significant role in the control of aggression" (Feshbach, 1983, p. 267). Indeed, a plethora of empirical investigations have found that empathy inhibits, or at least mitigates, aggressive and antisocial behaviours (Miller & Eisenberg, 1988). In addition to the critical role that empathy plays in helping individuals desist from aggressive behaviours, research also points to the significance of empathy in enhancing or diminishing the quality of one's social relationships (Schonert-Reichl, 1993). Empathy, according to some, is one of the most desirable of personality traits, not only because it provides a buffer against antisocial and aggressive behaviours, but also because of positive association with pro-social behaviours, such as helping, sharing and cooperating.

Although there has been increased theoretical and research attention aimed at delimiting the social–emotional factors that significantly impact children's psychological well-being and behavioural adjustment (Denham, 1998; Saarni, 1999), there has been relatively limited empirical attention given to intervention and prevention efforts that might support or increase emotional and social understanding during childhood (for exceptions, see Conduct Problems Research Group, 1999; Denham & Burton, 1996; Feshbach, 1979; Greenberg, Kusche, Cook, & Quamma, 1995). Notwithstanding the limited research, the promotion of social competence in schools has emerged as a focus during the past decade (Consortium on the School-Based Promotion of Social Competence, 1994; Durlak, 1995; Durlak & Wells, 1997; Schonert-Reichl & Hymel, 1996; Weissberg & Greenberg, 1998). Due, in part, to increased recognition that social–emotional factors are inextricably linked to such factors as childhood aggression, academic functioning and school drop-out, intervention and prevention programs designed to promote children's social competence and reduce aggression have grown progressively throughout the United States and Canada (Greenberg, Domitrovich, & Bumbarger, 2001; Miller et al., 1998). Prevention rather than intervention programs in particular have increased in popularity, in part due to a renewed focus on developmental resilience. Indeed, the last decade has witnessed a shift from a search for causal factors associated with the onset and escalation of mental health problems to a search for factors that foster desistance from antisocial behaviours over time. As noted by Durlak and Wells (1997), ". . . primary prevention in mental health may be defined as an intervention intentionally designed to reduce the future incidence of adjustment problems in currently normal populations as well as efforts directed at the promotion of mental health functioning" (p. 117). Recasting our priorities in terms of facilitating children's competence and not simply limiting risk extends our focus to all children, instead of just those exhibiting problems. Most relevant to our research is the notion that "potential exists to foster resilience through well-designed prevention programs particularly in major social institutions such as public schools"

(Doll & Lyon, 1998, p. 349). In contrast to other potential sites
for intervention, schools provide access to all children on a regular and consistent basis over the majority of their formative years
of personality development; thus the school environment can be
a fundamental locus of change (Elias et al., 1998). Nonetheless,
while a number of classroom and school-based programs have
been designed to promote children's social–emotional development, there is little extant research evaluating the effectiveness of
such programs (Miller, Brehm, & Whitehouse, 1998). Moreover,
there is scant longitudinal research directly assessing the long-
term impact of primary preventive social/emotional competence promotion programs on the trajectories of children's social
and emotional health.

ROE Goals and Theoretical Framework

The primary goals of ROE are threefold, namely to (1) develop
children's social and emotional understanding, (2) promote children's pro-social behaviours and decrease their aggressive behaviours, and (3) increase children's knowledge about human
development and effective parenting practices. The ROE curriculum model draws on current research and theory in developmental psychology that suggests that emotion processes and
social understanding play critical roles in children's interpersonal
relationships and social behaviours (Shipman, Zeman, Penza, &
Champion, 2000). More specifically, the ROE model draws from
theory and research aligned with the *functionalist* approach to emotions (Campos, Mumme, Kermoian, & Campos, 1994), wherein
emotion, understanding and expressivity are seen as playing central roles in the establishment and maintenance of children's
interpersonal relationships (Saarni, 1999). As well, the ROE
model's "roots" are founded on the belief that "emotions form the
motivational bases for empathy and pro-social behavior" (Izard,

Fine, Mostow, Trentacosta, & Campbell, 2002, p. 761). Empathy, in particular, is considered to be core to the ROE curriculum due to its centrality in the moral personality. Indeed, empathy has been identified as one of the most essential of personality traits because not only does empathy lead individuals to desist from aggression, but also the ability to empathize is positively associated with the development of positive social relationships and prosocial behaviours.

Researchers have grappled for years with finding ways to define and measure empathy. Norma Feshbach, a professor at UCLA who has been examining empathy for over three decades, has put forward a three-component model in which empathy is conceptualized as comprising both cognitive and emotional components. These three components include the ability to a) identify others' emotions, b) understand and explain other's emotions, and c) be emotionally responsive to others. These three components are necessary for empathy to emerge—in essence, these components are the roots of empathy. Feshbach's framework provides a conceptual basis for the content of the ROE lessons and an organizing scheme for the measures that we utilized in our evaluation design.

In keeping with other comprehensive social competence promotion programs, embedded within the ROE program are explicit components aimed at altering the ecology of the classroom environment to one in which belonging, caring, collaboration and understanding others are emphasized (Cohen, 2001). Throughout the program lessons, for instance, are opportunities for children to be engaged collaboratively in pro-social activities for the baby (e.g., singing and recording songs). Such activities, specifically those in which individuals work collectively on projects that benefit others, have been shown to promote altruism and a pro-social value orientation (Battistich et al., 1997; Staub, 1988).

Evaluations of the "Roots of Empathy" Program

To date, there have been four outcome studies examining the efficacy of ROE. These include an examination of the ROE's effectiveness with primary grade children, a national evaluation (including children in Vancouver and Toronto), a rural–urban evaluation, and a randomized controlled trial (RCT). These studies have been conducted by Dr. Kimberly Schonert-Reichl in collaboration with Dr. Clyder Hertzman and Dr. Veronica Smitt.

2000–2001 Primary Grade Evaluation of ROE

The first attempt to examine empirically the efficacy of the ROE was conducted in Vancouver in the 2000–2001 school year (Schonert-Reichl et al., 2005). This evaluation included 132 primary grade children (Grades 1 to 3) drawn from ten classrooms (five program, five comparison). Comparison classrooms were chosen to match with the program classrooms as closely as possible with respect to grade, gender and racial/ethnic composition (in the total sample, 61 per cent of the children had come from homes in which English was a second language). Instructors were trained in the ROE program and provided three lessons per month during the school year. A battery of measures assessing emotional and social understanding was individually administered to children at pre-test and post-test. To examine the impact of ROE on children's pro-social and aggressive behaviours, teachers rated each student at pre-test and post-test on several dimensions of social behaviour. Additionally, because of recent research indicating that aggression is multifaceted, three different dimensions of aggression were assessed. These included:

- *Proactive aggression—"cold-blooded" aggression.* Proactive aggression is described as *instrumental*—that is, a proactively aggressive child sees aggression as a viable way to obtain a resource (for example, an object, a privilege or a territory) or could be directed to another child with the explicit purpose of intimidating or dominating that child. Proactive aggression has often been considered to be synonymous with bullying.

- *Reactive aggression—"hot-headed" aggression.* Reactive aggression is typically seen as impulsive and occurs in response to a perceived threat or provocation.
- *Relational aggression*—also referred to as social aggression or indirect aggression. Relational aggression refers to harming others through purposeful manipulation or damage to their peer relationships through exclusion, gossiping, back-stabbing and the like.

Results revealed that children who had experienced the ROE program, compared to children who had not, were more advanced in their emotional and social understanding on almost all dimensions assessed. Developmental changes in children's socio-emotional knowledge were associated with concomitant reductions in aggressive behaviours and increases in pro-social behaviours (helping, sharing, cooperating). Most notably, while ROE program children significantly decreased in proactive aggression (an instrumental form of aggression associated with bullying) across the school year, comparison children demonstrated significant increases in this form of aggression. That is, children in the ROE were less likely to view aggression as an effective and viable means for obtaining social goals than were comparison children at post-test. Moreover, whereas ROE children evidenced a significant decrease in proactive aggression from pre-test to post-test, children in the comparison group demonstrated a significant increase in proactive aggression. Indeed, whereas 88 per cent of the ROE children who evidenced this form of aggression at pre-test decreased at post-test, only 9 per cent of the comparison children did so. Moreover, 50 per cent of the comparison children demonstrated an increase in proactive aggression from pre-test to post-test.

2002–2003 National Evaluation of ROE

The second ROE evaluation, conducted in 2001–2002, was a multi-site investigation and included 585 intermediate grade children (Grades 4 to 7) drawn from 28 classrooms (14 ROE classrooms, 14 comparison) across Canada (in Vancouver and Toronto). Again, ROE program classrooms were carefully matched with comparison classrooms on grade level, gender, race/ethnicity and teacher experience (53 per cent of the children were from homes in which English was a second language). Children completed measures assessing empathy and emotional understanding, and teachers assessed children's social behaviours with the same measure used in the previous evaluation. In response to concerns about bias in teachers' ratings of behaviours (it was suggested that teachers were not "blind" to intervention status—that is, teachers knew which children were getting the ROE program and which children were in the comparison classrooms), a measure of peers' nominations of children's pro-social and aggressive behaviours was also included.

The findings of this second study both replicated and extended the results of the initial evaluation study. More specifically, ROE program children, relative to comparison children, exhibited significant increases in emotional understanding and pro-social behaviours and significant decreases in aggressive behaviours. In accord with the findings from the first evaluation, for instance, whereas children who received the ROE program showed significant decreases in teachers' ratings of proactive aggression, comparison children exhibited significant increases in this type of aggression across the school year. In addition, ROE program children demonstrated significant decreases in teachers' reports of relational aggression. When changes were examined in only those children demonstrating some form of aggression at pre-test, for proactive aggression it was found that 67 per cent of ROE program children *decreased* at post-test whereas 64 per cent of comparison children *increased*. In regard to relational aggression a similar pattern emerged—there was a 61-per-cent decrease in relational aggression among ROE children and a 67-per-cent increase among comparison children.

Not only did teachers rate children in the ROE program as less aggressive at the end of the school year, but also other children saw their ROE peers as kinder and more pro-social. Specifically, children who received the ROE program were significantly more likely to have increases across the course of the school year in peer ratings of pro-social behaviours (sharing, helping, cooperating) and pro-social characteristics (kind, trustworthy, able to see others' perspectives) than children in the comparison classrooms.

2002–2003 Rural–Urban Evaluation

In the 2002 school year the evaluations of ROE were extended to include a study examining ROE effectiveness across rural and urban settings. The study sample included 419 intermediate grade children (Grades 4 to 7) drawn from rural and urban schools (10 ROE program classrooms, 10 comparison classrooms). Again, ROE classrooms were carefully matched with comparison classrooms on important variables, including grade, gender, race/ethnicity and teacher experience (30 per cent of the children were from homes in which English was a second language). In addition to assessing children's emotional understanding and social behaviours (as assessed by teachers and peers), this time measures were included assessing children's beliefs about parenting (e.g., parenting efficacy) along with a measure assessing classroom belonging and supportiveness.

The findings of this study both replicated and extended our previous investigations. There were positive and significant changes in teachers' ratings of ROE children's pro-social, relational and reactive aggression across the school year. Again, whereas ROE program children demonstrated significant improvements in these behaviours from pre-test to post-test, comparison children did not. As well, children who received the ROE program, in contrast to those children who did not, evidenced significant improvements in peer ratings of pro-social behaviours, pro-social characteristics and peer acceptance. That is, ROE children were not only seen as more kind and helpful than children in the comparison classrooms, but also were better liked by those in their own classrooms at the end of the school year. These shifts in ROE classrooms to becoming more caring environments are also demonstrated in the data examining classroom supportiveness. Children in ROE program classrooms showed significant increases in their assessments of classroom supportiveness and classroom autonomy (i.e., having a "voice" in the classroom) than children in comparison classrooms. These results support the ecological focus of the ROE program and underline the importance of creating classrooms in which caring about one another is emphasized. Also noteworthy are the findings regarding parenting efficacy— children who received the ROE program, in contrast to children in comparison classrooms, significantly and positively changed in their ability to see themselves as knowing what to do as a parent.

Evaluating Implementation

Implementation has frequently been described as "the degree to which the treatment is delivered as intended" or "what a program consists of in practice." Examining implementation of a program is essential to examining the effectiveness of a program. Nevertheless, implementation has infrequently been examined. For instance, Durlak (1997), in a review of social–emotional competence promotion programs, noted that only 5 per cent of 1,200 programs reviewed included some information on evaluation of implementation.

Implementation Promotion and Verification

There exist two components of implementation—implementation promotion and implementation verification. Implementation promotion includes all of those steps that program originators take to ensure accurate implementation of their program. Implementation verification refers to an evaluation of the degree to which the program was delivered as intended (e.g., dosage, program adherence, participant responsiveness).

Weissberg and Greenberg (1998), in their extensive review of school- and community-based prevention programs, indicate that programs with the highest degree of implementation promotion include the following characteristics: an underlying theoretical framework conveyed to implementers, high-quality pre-implementation instructor training, training and curriculum manuals, and on-site mentoring and support from school administration. In reviewing the steps that ROE has taken to promote sound and rigorous implementation, it is clear that they have included every one of the components espoused by Weissberg and Greenberg. Hence, ROE has the highest degree of implementation promotion.

Describing implementation promotion, however, is not enough. It is also important to examine systematically the quality of program implementation. In the 2001–2002 study examining ROE across Canada among children in Grades 4 to 7 this is exactly what was done. More specifically, to assess implementation dosage and quality, ROE instructors and teachers were asked to complete questionnaires assessing their implementation of the ROE program at pre-test and post-test.

Analyses revealed several interesting findings. First, with regard to program dosage—the number of lessons that each ROE instructor implemented to children—it was found that the average number of lessons taught among the fourteen instructors was 25.21, with a range of 23 to 26 lessons. Hence, it appears that the implementation dosage is very high across ROE instructors and classrooms.

The relations between dimensions of implementation and child outcomes were subsequently examined. The following findings emerged:

- Years of instructors' experience were associated with the degree of improvement in ROE children's knowledge of infant crying.
- Years of instructors' experience were also associated with significant reductions in teacher-rated relational aggression.
- ROE teachers' positive beliefs in the efficacy of the ROE program were associated with reductions in ROE children's proactive and relational aggression.
- Having previous experience delivering the ROE curriculum was significantly and positively associated with ROE children's advances in their knowledge of the emotional states associated with infant crying, and significantly associated with reductions in their relational and proactive aggression. This finding is in accord with that of previous research that indicated child outcomes were greater when an instructor/teacher had two to three years of experience teaching the program (Pepler, King, & Byrd, 1991).
- Children who were rated as more engaged during the ROE lesson (pre/post) had greater increases in knowledge of

emotions and infants' internal emotional states than those children rated as less engaged.

Taken together, these results provide some support for the importance of examining implementation integrity to determine the ways in which program delivery affects child outcomes.

Notes

CHAPTER I

1. Yau, Maria. "Roots of Empathy: Overall feedback from classroom teachers and students," Toronto: Roots of Empathy, 2003. In Maria Yau's research from 2003, 95 per cent of the students, from kindergarten to Grade 8, who participated in the Roots of Empathy program, choose the highest rating, "liked a lot", as their response to the baby visits.

2. McCain, Hon. Margaret Norrie, and Mustard, J. Fraser. "Early Years Study: Reversing the Real Brain Drain," Toronto: Publications Ontario, April 1999: 7.

3. Maytree Foundation is a private Canadian charitable foundation established in 1982. The Foundation is committed to reducing poverty and inequality in Canada and to building strong civic communities. The Foundation seeks to accomplish its objectives by identifying, supporting and funding ideas, leaders and leading organizations that have the capacity to make change and advance the common good. (Quote from the Maytree website: www.maytree.com).

4. Bettelheim, Bruno. *A Good Enough Parent: A Book on Child-rearing.* New York: Alfred A. Knopf, 1987.

5. Kohn, A. "Caring kids: The role of schools," *Phi Delta Kappan*, 72/7, 1991: 496–506. Gallo, D. "Educating for Empathy, Reason and Imagination," *The Journal of Creative Behavior*, 23/2, 1989: 98–115.

6. Schweinhart, L.J., Barnes, H.V., & Weikart D.P. "Significant benefits: The High/Scope Perry Preschool Study through age 27." In *Monographs of the High/Scope Educational Research Foundation*, Ypsilanti: High/Scope Press, 1993: 10.

7. Hoffman, M. L. *Empathy and Moral Development: Implications for Caring and Justice.* New York: Cambridge University Press, 2000.

CHAPTER 2

1. McCollough, T.E. *Truth and ethics in school reform*. Washington: Council for Educational Development and Research, 1992.

2. Ekman, P., Sorenson, E.R. & Friesen, W.V. "Pan-cultural elements in facial displays of emotions," *Science,* 164:875, 1969: 86-88. Study in which preliterate New Guinea tribes-people identified a number of emotional facial expressions in the same way that subjects in Japan, Brazil and the United States did.

3. Zahn-Waxler, C. & Yarrow, Radke M. "The development of altruism: Alternative research strategies." In *The Development of Prosocial Behavior*, ed., N. Eisenberg, New York: New York Academic Press, 1982.

4. Hoffman, Martin L. *Empathy and Moral Development: Implications for Caring and Justice*. New York: Cambridge University Press, 2000.

5. Eisenberg, Nancy. *The Caring Child*. Cambridge: Harvard University Press, 1992.

6. Five-year-old Kingsley Okuru fell to his death from his apartment balcony in Toronto at around 10:45 p.m. on June 5, 2004.

7. Olweus, D. *Bullying at School: What We Know and What We Can Do*. Cambridge: Blackwell, 1993.

8. Jones, B. F. "The New Definition of Learning: The First Step to School Reform." In *Restructuring to Promote Learning in America's Schools: A Guidebook,* Elmhurst: North Central Regional Educational Laboratory, 1990: 19.

CHAPTER 3

1. Denham, Susanne A. *Emotional Development in Young Children*. New York: The Guilford Press, 1998.

CHAPTER 5

1. Eliot, Lise. *What's Going on in There? How the Brain and Mind Develop in the First Five Years of Life*. New York: Bantam Books, 1999: 27.

2. Gopnik, Alison. *The Scientist in the Crib: Minds, Brains and How Children Learn*. New York: William Morrow & Co., 1999: 106.

3. Pollak, Seth D., & Kistler, Doris J. "Early experience is associated with the development of categorical representations for facial expressions of emotion," *Proceedings of the National Academy of Sciences USA*, 99:13, 2002: 9072-6.

4. Gunnar, M.R., & Nelson, C.A. "Event-related potentials in year-old infants predict negative emotionality and hormonal responses to separation," *Child Development*, 65, 1994: 80-94.

5. "The Early Years Study." See Chapter 1, note 2.

CHAPTER 6

1. Chess, S. & Thomas, A. *Know Your Child: An Authoritative Guide for Today's Parents*. New York: Basic Books, 1987.

2. *Ibid.*

3. Bourgeois, Paulette. *Franklin Has a Sleepover*. Toronto: Kids Can Press, 1996.

CHAPTER 7

1. Bowlby, John. *A Secure Base: Parent-Child Attachment and Healthy Human Development*. New York: Basic Books, 1988. Throughout this book, Bowlby references the extensive research on attachment conducted by Mary Ainsworth and Mary Main.

2. Shonkoff, Jack P. & Phillips, Deborah A., Eds. *From Neurons to Neighborhoods: The Science of Early Childhood Development*. Washington: National Academy Press, 2000: 225-266.

3. *Ibid.*

4. *Ibid.*

5. Bowlby, John. *A Secure Base: Parent-Child Attachment and Healthy Human Development*. New York: Basic Books, 1988.

CHAPTER 8

1. Sorce, J.F., et al. "Maternal emotional signaling: Its effect on the visual cliff behavior of 1-year-olds," *Developmental Psychology*, 21:1, 1985: 195-200.

2. Brazelton, Berry & Greenspan, Stanley. *The Irreducible Needs of Children*. New York: Perseus Books 2000: 121-122.

3. Greenberg, M. T., et al. "Promoting emotional competence in school-aged children: The effects of the PATHS curriculum," *Development and Psychopathology*, 7, 1995: 117-136.

4. Saarni, Carolyn. *The Development of Emotional Competence*. New York: The Guilford Series on Social and Emotional Development, 1999.

5. Kohn, A. "Caring Kids: The Role of the Schools," *Phi Delta Kappan*, 72/7, 1991: 496-506.

6. Gallo, D. "Educating for Empathy, Reason and Imagination," *The Journal of Creative Behavior*, 23:2, 1989: 98-115.

CHAPTER 9

1. Brazelton, Berry & Greenspan, Stanley. *The Irreducible Needs of Children*. New York: Perseus Books 2000: 148.

2. Kaiser Family Foundation, News Release re *Kids & Media @ The New Millennium*, November 17, 1999. www.kff.org

3. Children Now: "Tuned In or Tuned Out? America's Children Speak Out on the News Media", 1994. www.childrennow.org

CHAPTER 10

1. Glossop, Dr. Robert. "Interview: Dr. Robert Glossop of the Vanier Institute of the Family," *Link (Roots of Empathy Newsletter)*, 1:1, 2002:1.

2. Zeigler, S & Yau, M. "Do parenting and family literacy centres make a difference?" Toronto: Toronto District School Board Report, 2001.

3. Tremblay, R.E., et al. "Do children in Canada become more aggressive as they approach adolescence?" In *Growing up in Canada: National Longitudinal Survey of Children and Youth*, Human Resources Development Canada and Statistics Canada, Ottawa: Statistics Canada, 1996: 127-137.

CHAPTER 11

1. In January, 1999 in Manchester, England, eight-year-old Marie Bentham hanged herself in her bedroom with her skipping rope because she could no longer face the bullies at school.

2. In November 2000, Dawn-Marie Wesley, 14, of Mission, B.C. hanged herself shortly after phone calls from three teenage girls. Wesley's suicide note said that she had been threatened by bullies and she believed death was her only escape.

3. In April 2002, Emmet Fralick, a 14-year-old pupil at St. Agnes School in Halifax, Nova Scotia, shot himself in his bedroom because he was being bullied by classmates. Emmet was regarded as a quiet boy with a reputation for kindness to others.

4. Underwood, Marion K. *Social Aggression Among Girls*. New York: The Guilford Series on Social and Emotional Development, 2003.

5. Olweus, D. *Bullying at School: What We Know and What We Can Do*. Oxford: Blackwell, 1993.

6. Tremblay, R. E. et al. "Developmental trajectories of childhood disruptive behaviors and adolescent delinquency: A six site, cross-national study," *Developmental Psychology*, 39:2, 2003: 222-245.

7. "Bullying at School." See Chapter 11, note 5.

8. Baillargeon, R., Tremblay, R. E. & Willms, J. D. "Physical aggression among toddlers, does it run in families?" In *Vulnerable Children: Findings from Canada's National Longitudinal Survey of Children and Youth*. Ed. Willms, J.D. Edmonton: University of Alberta Press, 2002: 121-130.

CHAPTER 12

1. Connor, Sarah K. & McIntyre, Lynn. "The effects of smoking and drinking during pregnancy." In *Vulnerable Children: Findings from Canada's National Longitudinal Survey of Children and Youth*. Ed. Willms, J.D. Edmonton: University of Alberta Press, 2002: 131-145.

2. *Source: Canadian Council on Smoking and Health, 1993.*

3. *Source: Health Canada, Government of Canada, 1996.*

CHAPTER 13

1. Caprara, G.V., et al. "Prosocial foundations of children's academic achievement," *Psychological Science*, 11, 2000: 302-306.

2. Gardner, Howard. *Frames of Mind: The Theory of Multiple Intelligences.* New York: Basic Books, 1983.

CHAPTER 14

1. Cook, Cynthia & Willms, Douglas J. "Balancing Work and Family Life." In *Vulnerable Children: Findings from Canada's National Longitudinal Survey of Children and Youth.* Ed. Willms, J.D. Edmonton: University of Alberta Press, 2002: 183-197.

2. Eisenberg, Nancy. *The Caring Child.* Cambridge: Harvard University Press, 1992: 87 references the study of Oliner, S.P. & Oliner, P.M. "The Altruistic Personality: Rescuers of Jews in Nazi Europe." New York: Free Press, 1988.

CHAPTER 15

1. Roots of Empathy research, Appendix B: see page 239. Grateful acknowledgements to Kathleen Cotton for "Developing Empathy in Children and Youth", her report on empathy research, School Improvement Research Series, North West Regional Education Laboratory (2001).

APPENDIX A

1. *Statistics Canada (2000). Youth Court Statistics 1997-8.* Ottawa: Canadian Centre for Justice Statistics

APPENDIX B

1 Please note that UBC, under the direction of Drs. Kim Schonert-Reichl and Clyde Hertzman, is now the national repository of all ROE evaluations that take place across Canada and beyond. As well, Dr.

Hertzman is an advisory members of the ROE research board. Finally, the measures developed/chosen by Dr. Schonert-Reichl for all of the ROE evaluations conducted thus far in BC are being used in several ROE evaluations across Canada and in Japan and Australia.

References

Battistich, V., Solomon, D., Watson, M., & Schaps, E. 1997. "Caring school communities." *Educational Psychologist, 32,* 137-151.

Campos, J., Mumme, D., Kermoian, R., & Campos, R. 1994. "A functionalist perspective on the nature of emotion." *Monographs of the Society for Research in Child Development, 59* (2-3), 284-303.

Canadian Education Statistics Council. 2000. Education Indicators in Canada: Report of the Pan-Canadian Education Indicators Program 1999

Cohen, J., ed. 2001. *Caring Classrooms/Intelligent Schools: The Social Emotional Education of Young Children.* New York: Teachers College Press.

Conduct Problems Prevention Research Group. 1999. Initial impact of the fast track prevention trial for conduct problems: II. Classroom effects. *Journal of Consulting and Clinical Psychology, 67,648-657.*

Consortium on the School-based Promotion of Social Competence, 1994. "The school-based promotion of social competence: Theory, research, practice, and policy." In *Stress, Risk, and Resilience in Children and Adolescents: Processes, Mechanisms, and Interventions, eds.,* R.J. Haggerty, L.R. Sherrod, N. Garmezy, & M. Rutter, 268–316, New York, NY: Cambridge University Press.

Coie, J.D., & Dodge, K.A. 1998. "Aggression and antisocial behavior." In *Handbook of Child Psychology:* Vol. 3: *Social, Emotional, and Personality Development*, 5th ed., W. Damon and N. Eisenberg, 779-862. New York: Wiley.

Cook, E.T., Greenberg, M.T., & Kusché, C.A. 1994. "The relations between emotional understanding, intellectual functioning, and disruptive behavior problems in elementary school aged children." *Journal of Abnormal Child Psychology, 22,* 205-219.

Denham, S.A. 1998. *Emotional Development in Young Children.* New York: Guilford.

Denham, S.A., & Burton, R. 1996. "A social-emotional intervention program for at-risk four-year-olds." *Journal of School Psychology, 34,* 224-245.

Dodge, K.A., & Coie, J.D. 1987. "Social-information processing factors in reactive and proactive aggression in children's peer groups." *Journal of Personality and Social Psychology, 53,* 1146-1158.

Doll, B., & Lyon, M.A. 1998. "Risk and resilience: Implications for the delivery of educational and mental health services in schools." *School Psychology Review,* 27, 348-363.

Dryfoos, J.G. 1990. *Adolescents at Risk: Prevalence and Prevention.* New York: Oxford University Press.

Durlak, J.A. 1995. *School-based Prevention Programs for Children and Adolescents.* Thousand Oaks, CA: Sage.

Durlak, J.A. 1997. *Successful Prevention Programs for Children and Adolescents.* New York: Plenum Press.

Durlak, J.A., & Wells, A.M. 1997. "Primary prevention mental health programs for children and adolescents: A meta-analytic review." *American Journal of Community Psychology* 25, 115–152.

Eisenberg, N., & Miller, P.A., 1987. "The relation of empathy to prosocial and related behaviors. *Psychological Bulletin,* 101, 91–119.

Elias, M.J., Zins, J.E., Weissberg, K.S., Greenberg, M.T., Haynes, N.M., Kessler, R., Schwab-Stone, M.E., & Shriver, T.M. 1998. *Promoting Social and Emotional Learning: Guidelines for Educators* Alexandria, VA: Association for Supervision and Curriculum Development.

Farrington, D.P. 1991. "Childhood aggression and adult violence: Early precursors and later-life outcomes." In *The Development and Treatment of Childhood Aggression,* ed., D.J. Pepler & R.K. Rubin, 5-29. Hillsdale, NJ: Erlbaum.

Farrington, D.P. 1992. "Explaining the beginning, progress, and ending of antisocial behavior from birth to adulthood." In *Facts, frameworks and forecasts: Advances in criminological theory,* vol. 3, ed., J. McCord, 253–286. New Brunswick, NJ: Transaction.

Feshbach, N.D. 1979. "Empathy training: A field study in affective education." In *Aggression and Behavior Change: Biological and Social Processes,* ed., S. Feshbach & Fraczek, 234-249. New York: Praeger.

Feshbach, N.D. 1983. "Learning to care: A positive approach to child training and discipline." *Journal of Clinical Child Psychology,* 12 (3), 266–271.

Greenberg, M.T., Domitrovich, C., & Bumbarger, B. 2001. "The prevention of mental disorders in school-aged children: Current state of the field." *Prevention & Treatment, 4,* 1–48.

Greenberg, M.T., Kusché, C. A., Cook, E.T., & Quamma, J.P. 1995. "Promoting emotional competence in school-aged children: The effects of the PATHS curriculum." *Development and Psychopathology, 7,* 117–136.

Hoffman, M.L. 1981. "Is altruism part of human nature?" *Journal of Personality & Social Psychology,* 40 (1), 121–137.

Institute of Medicine. 1994. *Reducing Risks for Mental Disorders: Frontiers for Preventative Intervention Research.* Washington, D.C.

Izard, C.E., Fine, S., Mostow, A., Trentacosta, C., & Campbell, J. 2002. "Emotional processes in normal and abnormal development and preventive intervention." *Developmental and Psychopathology, 14,* 761–787.

Loeber, R., Wung, P., Keenan, K. & Giroux, B. 1993. "Parameters influencing social problem-solving of aggressive children." In *Advances in Behavioural Assessment of Children and Families: A Research Annual,* vol. 5, ed., R.J. Ping, 31–63. London: Kingsley.

Miller, P.A., Brehm, K., & Whitehouse, S. 1998. "Reconceptualizing school-based prevention for antisocial behavior within a resiliency framework." *School Psychology Review, 27,* 364–379.

Miller, P A., & Eisenberg, N. 1988. "The relation of empathy to aggressive and externalizing/antisocial behaviors." *Psychological Bulletin, 103,* 324–344.

National Advisory Mental Health Council. 1990. National Plan for Research on Child and Adolescent Mental Disorders (DHHS Publication No. 90-1683). Washington, DC: U.S. Department of Health and Human Services.

Organization for Economic Co-operation and Development. 1995. Our Children at Risk.

Offer, D., & Schonert-Reichl, K.A. 1992. "Debunking the myths of adolescence: Findings from recent research. *Journal of the American Academy of Child and Adolescent Psychiatry, 31,* 1003–1014.

Offord, D.R., Boyle, M., & Racine, Y.A. 1991. "The epidemiology of antisocial behavior in childhood and adolescence. In *Development and Treatment of Childhood Aggression,* eds., D.J. Pepler & K.H. Rubin, 31–52. Hillsdale, NJ: Erlbaum.

Parke, R.D., & Slaby, R.G. 1983. "The development of aggression." In *Handbook of Child Psychology: vol. 4, Personality and Socialization Processes*, 547–641, ed., E.M. Hetherington, 4th ed. New York: Wiley.

Patterson, G.R. 1993. "Orderly change in a stable world: The antisocial trai as a chimera." *Journal of Consulting and Clinical Psychology, 61, 911-919.*

Pepler, D.J., King, G., & Byrd, W. 1991. "A social-cognitively based social skills training program for aggressive children." In *Development and Treatment of Childhood Aggression*, eds., D.J. Pepler & K.H. Rubin, 361–379. Hillsdale, NJ: Erlbaum.

Romano, E., Tremblay, R. E., Vitaro, F., Zoccolillo, M., & Pagani, L. 2001. "Prevalence of psychiatric diagnosis and the role of perceived impairment: Findings from an adolescent community sample." *Journal of Child Psychology and Psychiatry, 42, 451–461.*

Saarni, C. 1999. *The Development of Emotional Competence.* New York: Guilford.

Schonert-Reichl, K.A. 1993. "Empathy and social relationships in adolescents with behavioral disorders." *Behavioral Disorders, 18, 189–204.*

Schonert-Reichl, K.A., & Hymel, S. 1996. "Promoting social development and acceptance in the elementary classroom." In *Teaching Students with Diverse Needs*, ed., J. Andrews, 152–200, Toronto, Canada: Nelson Canada.

Schonert-Reichl, K.A., Smith, V., Zaidman-Zait, A., 2005. *Effects of the "Roots of Empathy" Program on Children's Emotional and Social Competence.* Manuscript submitted for publication.

Shipman, K., Zeman, J., Penza, S., & Champion, K. 2000. "Emotion management skills in sexually maltreated and nonmaltreated girls: A developmental psychopathology perspective." *Development and Psychopathology, 12, 47–62.*

Steinhauer, P.D. 1996. *Developing Resiliency in Children from Disadvantaged Populations.* Ottawa: National Forum on Youth.

Staub, E. 1988. "The evolution of caring and nonaggressive persons and societies." *Journal of Social Issues, 44, 81–100.*

Weissberg, R.P., & Greenberg, M.T. 1998. School and community competence-enhancement and prevention programs. In *Handbook of child psychology: vol.5. Child psychology in practice*, ed., I.E. Siegel & K.A. Renninger. 877–954, 5th ed. New York: Wiley.